CW01508743

NAMAN

THE
HITMAN
THE **ROHIT SHARMA** STORY

Vijay Lokapally
G. Krishnan

BLOOMSBURY
NEW DELHI • LONDON • OXFORD • NEW YORK • SYDNEY

BLOOMSBURY INDIA
Bloomsbury Publishing India Pvt. Ltd
Second Floor, LSC Building No. 4, DDA Complex, Pocket C – 6 & 7,
Vasant Kunj, New Delhi 110070

BLOOMSBURY, BLOOMSBURY PRIME and the Diana logo are
trademarks of Bloomsbury Publishing Plc

First published in 2020

Copyright © Vijay Lokapally and G. Krishnan, 2020

Vijay Lokapally and G. Krishnan have asserted their right under the Indian
Copyright Act to be identified as the Authors of this work

All rights reserved. No part of this publication may be reproduced or trans-
mitted in any form or by any means, electronic or mechanical, including
photocopying, recording, or any information storage or retrieval system,
without prior permission in writing from the publishers

Bloomsbury Publishing Plc does not have any control over,
or responsibility for, any third-party websites referred to or in this book.
All internet addresses given in this book were correct at the time of going
to press. The author and publisher regret any inconvenience caused if
addresses have changed or sites have ceased to exist, but can accept
no responsibility for any such changes

ISBN: 978-93-90077-14-4

2 4 6 8 10 9 7 5 3 1

Photo credit: Bollywood Hungama (pp. 15-16 in photo section)

Printed and bound in India by Replika Press Pvt. Ltd

To find out more about our authors and books, visit
www.bloomsbury.com and sign up for our newsletters

For Sunanda and Akshay Lokapally,
my biggest critics and supporters.
The North Stand Gang of Wankhede Stadium,
the greatest fans of cricket on this planet.
— Vijay Lokapally

I dedicate this book to all those frontline warriors
who have sacrificed their lives to protect us.
To all my teachers, former cricketers and colleagues,
who have been kind to me and,
finally, to all the fans of Rohit Sharma.
— G. Krishnan

Contents

Foreword

It gives me great pleasure to write about Rohit Sharma, the Don of Borivali, as I often tease him. The more I see him, the more I am convinced that he has something very big in store for him. We all know he is an explosive batsman, an entertainer of the top grade, but how many of you know he is a very soft person, a kind-hearted man, who has always placed the team above himself?

For a middle order batsman to establish himself as one of world's premier openers is some achievement. He is not the first to have graduated to open the innings after starting as a middle order batsman. Sachin Tendulkar and Virender Sehwag are shining examples. In Rohit's case, he has left a huge impression with his big scores.

I have been closely associated with him from the 2007 World T20, which we won in South Africa. He played a very impactful innings at No. 6. His 30 not out was so critical when you look at the result. He went to bat in the 16th over and tore the bowling apart in his 16-ball knock. I was convinced that day he was a big-match player.

I remember vividly the tour to South Africa in 2011. The pitches in South Africa were quick, and Dale Steyn and Morne Morkel were spitting fire. We were without Gautam Gambhir, and Sachin Tendulkar was injured in the second match. The team needed an opener, and Rohit put his hand up. Mind you, he was not doing well, but I loved his courage. He showed the eagerness to open. To me, that decision to open, that failure, was his stepping stone to success.

We always knew he had awesome talent to play the white ball. I am not suggesting that he was not good with the red ball! His first two innings in Tests were centuries. But he always wanted to open the innings in all formats. His inspirations were Tendulkar and Sehwag. His promotion from middle order to opener has got him this far.

He has proved us right by emerging as the best one-day batsman. His authority at the crease is supreme. Also, I think he is the best player of the short ball—count the number of cuts, hooks and pulls that he executes in an innings. He has a splendid balance, which adds to his lazy elegance. I am amazed at the time he has to play the ball. He appears lazy, but just look at the time he has to play the ball.

Often Rohit is targeted by teammates who find him funny. He is not. He is very intense with his cricket. But yes, sometimes he comes up with funny questions. Just like me. People often thought I asked funny questions. We share a few qualities, I think. We have both had our ups and downs, and we both never had any support when we needed it. Rohit has always played in the team on the basis of his performances and not sought favours from the people who matter. I have sat out in Tests an entire season. So has Rohit. My cancer also hit my Test career, and that's why I see my journey through him. Red ball cricket is the toughest form of the game, and I want Rohit to play another 40 Tests or so.

Rohit is a very jovial character and fun to be with. From the time I have known him, he has not changed a bit. I have seen people change with time and success, but not Rohit. He has remained grounded, the same person I saw in our first season together. I don't like to disturb people, but I love speaking to Rohit regularly on his cricket. He has the best support at home, Ritika, who is my rakhi sister. They make a great couple.

I am sure Rohit will be India's most crucial player at the next T20 and 50-over World Cup. I want him to look after his fitness because Indian cricket needs him to be at his best.

I am so happy that Vijay Lokapally and G. Krishnan have come together to bring this book on the most exciting batsman of current times. I have known Vijay bhai from the time I made my first-class debut, and I know he and Krishnan will do justice to the subject. Vijay bhai is a rare journalist who understands cricket and cricketers so well. I wish him and Krishnan the best in this venture.

October 2020   – **Yuvraj Singh**

Acknowledgements

Paul Vinay Kumar believes in me more than I do myself. He convinced me to take up this project, and I accepted it to justify his faith in me. He has been the most important influence on me from the time I signed up to write the book on Virat Kohli. Next was *World Cup Warriors*, and now this. Thanks Paul, for all the support.

I am thankful to Rajiv Beri, the Managing Director of Bloomsbury. He trusted me to deliver the book on time. During the dark times of the COVID-19 pandemic, he was sure the story of Rohit Sharma would be a positive experience for all of us.

Aurodeep Mukherjee, our editor, has been a vital part of this journey and deserves huge credit for cleansing the manuscript.

Post retirement, I have found Ayon Sengupta, the dynamic Editor of *Sportstar*, a tremendous source of encouragement. Thanks to him, and V.V. Rajasekhar Rao, I have remained as busy as always. I also put on record the support I have received from K.C. Vijaya Kumar, the considerate Sports Editor of *The Hindu*.

One man who continues to stand by me like a rock is my childhood friend Ghaus Mohammad. He is my greatest motivator, and I owe it to him for keeping me focused during some very depressing phases of the pandemic. And my brother Ajay, who is an avid lover of the game, with sound knowledge of it too.

My colleagues for life—K.P. Mohan, Kamesh Srinivasan, Rakesh Rao, Y.B. Sarangi, C. Rajshekhar Rao, Manoj Vatsyayana, G. Rajaraman, R. Kaushik, Nilesh Mehta, V.V. Krishnan, Dwarkanath Sanzgiri, Vinayak Dalvi, K.V. Prasad, Mona Parthsarthi, Rajender Sharma, Kamal Sharma, Ziya Us Salam, V.V. Subrahmanyam—share my joy in this hard work, which has derived quotes and information from reports in *The Hindu*, *Sportstar*, *India Today* and Cricinfo.

I have also benefited from critical inputs provided by Charudutt Prabhu, a brilliant student of the game and a promising cricket writer.

I have my greatest well-wishers in A. Vishwambar Rao, Smita Rao, and their daughter A. Alekhya Rao, who is currently studying in Italy to become an architect. I am indebted to Sunanda and Akshay for putting up with my swinging moods as I concentrated on finishing the book at the cost of attending to work at home. They ensured I stuck to the deadline.

I also remember my late parents, Narayan Rao and Sarla, on all my happy occasions. They have created these moments for me.

My dear nephew, Shravan Nair, and niece, Shruti Mukundan, their parents, P.G. Mukundan and Kumud, will take pride in this effort of mine.

Last, but not the least, I am grateful to fellow author, the ever-smiling G. Krishnan, fondly called 'Gikku'. A wonderful human being, I look forward to working on more projects with him.

Dear readers, hope Gikku and I do not disappoint you.

— Vijay Lokapally

I am thankful to Paul Vinay Kumar, our publisher, for ensuring we meet the deadline, and the MD of Bloomsbury India Rajiv Beri for having faith in us.

Among the many who have played crucial roles in my growth as a sports journalist are my grandparents, late T.G. Suryanarayanan and Vasantha, in whose care I grew up in Chennai. I owe a lot to them for encouraging me to give up Chartered Accountancy to pursue a career in sports journalism.

My journey would not have been possible without the encouragement of my parents, G.K. Guruvayoorappan and Geetha, who always blessed me to do what I chose to. My father, in particular, has been my biggest critic.

The roles of my wife, Priya, and son, Aman, are huge. They helped me stay focused when writing this book and have always supported my interest in sports and my work.

I am thankful to my younger brother, late G. Chandrasekhar, who wanted me to write a book based on my experiences. I miss that he's no longer with us to see. 'GC' would have been proud of me!

I am thankful to my first Sports Editor, Joseph Hoover, who gave me the break in *Deccan Herald*. I would like to acknowledge the immense roles played by senior journalists and dear friends, R. Kaushik and G. Viswanath.

I am grateful to Rohit's friends Abhishek Nayar, his India teammate from the Under-19 days, Manoj Tiwary, and his childhood coach, Dinesh Lad, for their insightful revelations.

Also a big thank you to Sachin Tendulkar, Yuvraj Singh, Harbhajan Singh, Zaheer Khan, Cheteshwar Pujara and Shikhar Dhawan for their support.

I am thankful to Vijay Lokapally for believing in me and asking me to be a part of this book. His guidance in my career has been immense.

This would not have been complete without the wonderful editing by Aurodeep Mukherjee.

– G. Krishnan

Introduction

There should not be any comparisons. Rohit Sharma reminds one of Virender Sehwag. Rohit has all the time like Mark Waugh to play the ball. Rohit is as aggressive in the middle as Virat Kohli. Rohit can match the stroke play of Steve Smith. The fact is that Rohit alone can bat like Rohit. Let us accept the fact that there is not a batsman like him, who doesn't compromise his style in any format of the game.

He has style, skill and attitude. These are essential attributes that have shaped careers in every era of cricket. Someone like Viv Richards believed there was not a bowler who could intimidate him. Sunil Gavaskar's strength came from his impeccable technique that helped him perform on all kinds of challenging surfaces. Rohit subscribes to both these philosophies.

Give him a target, and he will rise to the task with the confidence of a master. He may fail at times, but not for want of effort. He was rightly criticised on various occasions for throwing his wicket, but then he has done well not to allow those rough phases to impact his approach to the game.

When he received his Test cap from Sachin Tendulkar at the Eden Gardens in 2013, it was in the final season of the maestro. In a fine symbolic moment, Tendulkar passed on the mantle to Rohit. True, they had their own ways of accumulating runs, but it was interesting when Tendulkar once tagged Rohit and tweeted, 'Would be fun to open with you.' They have never opened the innings for India or Mumbai Indians.

One innings that convinced Tendulkar that Rohit was the batsman for the future came against South Africa at Visakhapatnam in October 2019, when he slammed 176 and 127. In an interview with *India Today*, Tendulkar said these glowing words about Rohit, 'For me, the turning point was when he decided to step down the track to negate (Vernon) Philander's swing. As it is, he was batting outside the crease. Till then Philander had bowled three good overs to him. He reduced the distance and forced him to change his line and length. South Africa was then forced to ask the wicketkeeper to come up. That's one thing the fast bowler never enjoys. The bowler gets distracted and, I think, Rohit forced Philander to distraction. It was a game-changing moment. After that we know Rohit's class. The way he batted, his front foot defence, the manner in which he began to defend with a long stride forward, that was special. Once a batsman of Rohit's calibre gets going, it's difficult to stop him. Watching Rohit's batting always becomes fun.'

Such approval of Rohit's symphony at the crease by a legend is the final stamp of approval on his awesome talent.

There is a certain charm about Rohit's batting. To begin with, he defies the Bombay school of thought. He does not believe in compiling runs—he plunders them. He takes the bowlers by the scruff of their neck and dictates his terms. He is not the one to wait and strike. He does not believe in conceding the stage to the bowlers to come to terms with the pitch. Sehwag always advocated his policy of 'ball is meant to be hit'. And Rohit has followed it in every format.

Nimble footwork and skilled wristwork can prove a lethal combination. The ease with which Rohit is able to find gaps comes from his reliance on wristwork, where he plays the ball late and into areas unmanned. Setting a field for Rohit can prove a nightmare for any captain. The bowlers often come to grief because Rohit manages to alter his initial movement. A drive, in a flash, can become a cut, or a late cut, as his excellent eye and footwork ensure he is in the best position to hit the ball.

As Tendulkar says, Rohit's 'bat swing' is an amazing asset in his repertoire. It is as if Rohit plans his innings the night before, conjuring situations and simulating his response. The nonchalance is not to be missed. A caress, and the ball is flying to the boundary, eager to escape the wrath of Rohit's bat. He does have some robust shots to display, but the shots he plays so softly are the ones that take your breath away.

Is batting a war? Modern critics tend to believe so. The batsman wanting to give the bowler a charge. The bowler retaliating with a glare or a short ball. The batsman trying to match the aggression and falling into the trap. Not Rohit. He is convinced that it is a mind game where the bowler tries to read the batsman's moves. It can be an intriguing contest whenever it involves a batsman of Rohit's calibre. He knows when to stay cool and when to explode.

He plays the good innings in his mind, quite like Virat, who loves to relive the great moments in the middle. The best thing about Rohit is he loses little time in calculating his ability in that particular session, to survive or thrive by attacking. His basic technique is sound, and he has, over the years, come to hone his stroke play to the benefit of the team.

Rohit's ball sense can be as good as any other batsman in contemporary cricket—the sense to leave the ball when the seam and swing are alarming. Of course there is room for improvement, but Rohit makes no claims to being a perfect batsman. Most receptive to criticism, he has come to understand that there is no substitute for hard work on the field. You can experiment in practice sessions, but to put something in practice during matches is an art. Rohit is in an ongoing process in acquiring that art to suit his style of batsmanship.

The sound of the ball hitting Rohit's bat is melody. His timing is the supreme factor of his run-making quality. His ability to learn from watching others is exemplary. He watches, learns and then executes the lessons at the appropriate time. 'I have seen him compile his runs like an acknowledged composer creating bewitching music,' asserts Kapil Dev, who confesses he is a fan of these modern cricketers who play far more entertaining cricket.

From his stance, movement of feet, to his follow-through to a shot, Rohit presents an aesthetic picture. He has been praised for his 'lazy elegance' at different times by different commentators.

His batting is elegance, pure elegance, with minimum effort. That's the reason for Rohit being able to produce those long innings—he is a champion at preserving energy.

His stroke play draws strength from his outstanding footwork. In his case, the lofted drive is quite a productive shot. He picks the line early and is at his devastating best against the medium-pacers, fully utilising the momentum of the ball. The back-lift and the follow-through of his bat rekindle memories of the grace that marked Greg Chappell's style, eyes focused fiercely on the ball and the head still. He is also adept at reaching the pitch of the ball to get maximum benefits from his effort.

Muhammad Ali in the ring, Michael Jordan on the court, Mark Spitz in the pool were all sights to behold. When Rohit strikes the ball with ease and perfection, it can be a blissful experience for the cricket fan and sends the stadium into raptures. Connoisseurs who have grown up on Gavaskar and G.R. Viswanath painting the cricket canvas with aesthetic value do not despair when Rohit sometimes comes up with a crass stroke—he is allowed that occasional indulgence.

Most great openers will tell you that their essential job is to see off the new ball. This can be done by adopting an aggressive approach or playing the defensive game. Rohit combines the two aspects of batting in Test matches but gets cracking in limited overs matches. He delights his teammates and the crowd by getting down to the business of making runs from the first ball itself.

Rohit has all the shots. His forceful play square of the wicket is a response to the length of the ball, the decision taken to the best of his abilities, often to fruitful use. There have been disappointing moments and phases too, but Rohit has managed to overcome them and plan his career. He is a typical modern cricketer who takes failures in his stride only to come back stronger.

He has come a long way from the brash youngster that he was. In an anecdote related by journalist Amol Karhadkar in *Sportstar*, Rohit and his friends got into a fight in Mumbai in peak traffic hours, bringing things to a stop. His car had brushed another car and the occupants had almost come to blows. That was a few months after India had won the 2007 T20 World Cup. Thankfully, the incident was closed without hurting Rohit's reputation. He may reflect and laugh on that evening on a Mumbai road today, but it taught him to be responsible in public life. There were youngsters who looked up to Rohit, and he had to set an example as a sporting hero.

The amazing talent that makes Indian cricket the hottest property in the world draws inspiration from the success stories scripted by the likes of Rohit. Is there a statute on judging the limits of an achiever? Certainly not, when the subject is someone like Rohit, who has succeeded in charting a journey for himself even when confronted with treacherous terrain. He has always pushed himself to reach the summit. If he is among the elite of international batting today, the credit lies with his ceaseless devotion to cricket.

Coaches point out the alacrity with which Rohit executes a shot as his forte. His trademark is the pull shot played with the passion of an achiever, which paints the most stunning image on a canvas scrutinised by the best in business. His drives on the rise are craftwork of the highest class. Rohit is the personification of a modern warrior who leaves nothing to his colleagues.

When challenged, Rohit can build an innings, clean and well-structured, confidently garnering runs. The team management and selectors have been grooming him to finish the job and look to become one of the most consistent performers. He abhors losing his wicket and has emerged a delightful batsman who shows no sign of fatigue even as he compiles runs, not just with fours and sixes, but ones and twos as well.

Rohit is the best ambassador for Indian cricket's excellent grooming structure. He rose through the ranks, shining as a junior cricketer, and put the experience to rich use in the senior grade. Self-analysis helped him grow mentally strong, meeting the demands of modern cricket as a champion.

In the post-Tendulkar era, Indian cricket has gained from some stellar contributions by Virat Kohli and Cheteshwar Pujara in the Test arena. Batsmen like K.L. Rahul, Rishabh Pant, Prithvi Shaw and Hanuma Vihari have shown the promise to keep alive the legacy of the Fab Five—Tendulkar, Rahul Dravid, Virender Sehwag, V.V.S. Laxman, Sourav Ganguly—by performing consistently in all conditions. Rohit is an integral part of this wonderful bunch as India looks to make history by excelling away from home. The responsibility is huge, but there is reason to believe in these quality cricketers.

Rohit currently stands at a critical stage of his career. He has developed his awesome run-scoring prowess from observing the seniors. Failures don't bog him down. Like Gavaskar, Tendulkar and Kohli, he has learnt to draw strength from the failures and setbacks he has faced and endured as expectations have increased manifold. He is always ready in battle gear, ready to fight, to hit back. No wonder his teammates love to call him 'The Hitman'. He has the eyes of an Argus to deal with challenges. For the benefit of Indian cricket, he has the ideal attitude to deliver. His motto, not to brood over anything, is just the mantra the team needs to move forward, riding on his strong and able shoulders.

ONE

Sachin Goes, Rohit Arrives

His arrival coincided with Sachin Tendulkar's departure. The two-match Test series against the West Indies was all about Tendulkar and was dubbed one of the most fascinating farewell series of all time. True, the world had seemed to stop to hail Donald Bradman when he made his final appearance just short of his 40th birthday on the 1948 tour to England. Tendulkar was as much an icon of the game as the greatest ever. Just as years of occupying the crease had taken its toll on Bradman's body, Tendulkar, as human as the Australian, had begun to feel the need to take a call on his future in the game.

From the time the West Indies were picked as the opposition to contest Tendulkar's farewell series, it was also known that the focus would be on the little master of modern cricket. Not since Sunil Gavaskar had an individual come to dominate batting as Tendulkar had. It was obvious that Tendulkar was to be the talk of the series, and there was little pressure on Rohit Sharma when he was picked to make his debut at the Eden Gardens in a match that lasted three days starting 6 November 2013. Rohit was not required to bat on the opening day, when the West Indies was bowled out for 234. The next day was to be an important one for his career.

Rohit was in a relaxed frame of mind when India began their innings. Off-spinner Shane Shillingford struck three blows and India was reduced to 82 for 4 when Rohit stepped on the turf to play his first innings in a Test six years after his ODI debut (against Ireland at Belfast in 2007). As Rohit and Tendulkar crossed each other on the field, a new era was ushered in. The 26-year-old was going to make his mark and step into history books with a century on debut to join an illustrious bunch of batsmen.

A Test match at the Eden Gardens can bring out the best in a cricketer. The ambience of the venue and the passionate support from the galleries is a thrilling combination for any player. Rohit was no exception. His gait to the middle was relaxed, indicating that he had prepared himself mentally to take over the mantle and transform himself into a batsman of substance. While it helped that all the focus was on Tendulkar, he had joined his partner Virat Kohli at a challenging time. Once he took the guard, Rohit understood that he had to seize this opportunity. He just could not afford a failure after having waited so long to play his first Test.

A run had been added to the scoreboard when Rohit lost Kohli. At 83 for 5, India was not really a happy dressing room. But Rohit knew his job well. With Mahendra Singh Dhoni for company, he lost little time in launching an eventful career with a century. For statistical-minded cricket fans, he was the 14th Indian to register a century on Test debut. However, he was evaluated differently by the experts of the game, who saw in him a potentially explosive batsman who promised to serve the team long, given his talent to easily execute difficult tasks.

The earliest indication of Rohit's amazing ability to bat with consummate ease had come at Udaipur in the 2006 Deodhar Trophy final at the Maharana Bhupal College ground. It was a 50-over game, and North Zone was the crowd favourite, especially after it had set a target of 279. West Zone, riding on Rohit's majestic knock of 142 not out off 123 balls (14x4, 3x6), made a mockery of the chase. West lost just two wickets as Rohit tore into the attack that included Gagandeep Singh, Joginder Sharma, Reetinder Sodhi and Abid Nabi, all tipped to play for India.

The MB College ground has an interesting history. The foundation of the ground was laid by Kapil Dev, one of India's greatest cricketers, in 1987. Rohit was not even born at the time. Nineteen years before Rohit played that magical innings, the citizens of Udaipur had been deeply disappointed by the Reliance World Cup preparatory camp being shifted due to poor pitches. It had left a scar on the organisational abilities of the home officials. 'It was a black day for us and we had worked hard to make amends,' remembered Mahender Sharma, an Udaipur Cricket Association official who rose to become the secretary of the Rajasthan Cricket Association.

After the match, Sharma added on behalf of his team, 'Rohit has erased those bitter memories for us.' Rohit indeed brought joy to the hosting unit with a spectacular performance. Observers remembered the fluency that marked Rohit's stroke play, particularly the ease with which he played the inside-out shots, reminding old-timers of the stylish G.R. Viswanath and Mohammad Azharuddin. His batting was a revelation that day, and even his opponents acknowledged Rohit's dazzling knock. The captain of the North Zone team, Dinesh Mongia, made a prophetic comment when he said, 'This boy will play long. He is destined for much greater deeds.' And what made Mongia say that? 'His timing and the range of shots.'

So, timing it was when Rohit crafted that century at Eden Gardens. Was there a shot where the ball did not go where he intended it to? Not one. Rohit was in complete control, toying with the West Indian bowlers, his 177 off 301 balls a mini masterclass. Critics noted that it was a perfect preview of Rohit's talent on the big stage, his ability to adapt and dominate, much to the delight of the spectators and, more importantly, of the selectors, who felt they had made the Rohit selection at the right time. He had been maintaining a first-class average of 60-plus, and a few weeks prior to the Test series, he had slammed a 209 against Australia in an ODI.

Rajinder Singh Hans, member of the selection committee which picked Rohit to play against the West Indies after 108 appearances for India in ODIs, said, 'He had been scoring consistently at the domestic level. He was a much-feared batsman and we knew he had the capacity to play big innings. We had to give him a break and the selection committee felt it was the best time to give him a break. Sachin was on the verge of saying goodbye and the team needed a solid batsman in the middle order. We were unanimous that Rohit was the man to do the job. I am happy he proved us right.'

In terms of experience, Rohit was at the right stage.

Among the spectators was former Test opener Pranab Roy. He remarked, 'It was so pleasing to watch him play. His balance and timing were outstanding. The pitch was a difficult one. But he made it so easy. He has really matured into a fine player.' It suited Rohit that the pitch demanded utmost application and discipline. He knew he had to grab the chance since it had come after lot of hard work.

After his sensational innings, an elated Rohit said, 'I am very happy to score on debut. A Test hundred is special. The wicket was really slow. Once the ball got older, it was not coming on. You got to hold back strokes and play late. Playing on the rise was not an ideal option on this wicket. There was a time three years ago when nothing was going right. Being a sportsman, there is a lot of inspiration to take from so many sportspersons from around the world. I knew once I get an opportunity, I would try and make the most of it. I just waited… kept working on my game.'

It was a long wait for Rohit and credit to his dedication and tenacity. His journey is reminiscent of Marvan Atapattu of Sri Lanka, who made the most disastrous start to his career in 1990 but recovered to sign off as one of the finest to have graced his team. His scores in the first five Tests read 0, 0, 0, 1, 0, 0, 25, 22, 0, 25. This was over a period of seven years. He was practically written off after such a miserable run. In 1997, he smashed a classy century against India at Mohali, and his career took off on a rousing note. He finished his journey in 2007 with 16 centuries, including six double centuries, with a knock of 80 in his final innings. Rohit could have drawn his motivation from Atapattu, who got a break, struggled, lost his place, continued to fight and eventually made it big. As far as Rohit was concerned, he may not have started off on a poor note, but he did lose his place in the side, at times, playing poor shots, often called 'irresponsible' by the critics.

A second century in succession at Mumbai meant Rohit had played to his expectations and he could look forward to a long presence in the Indian team. While his game was overshadowed by Tendulkar's farewell, Cheteshwar Pujara, who also scripted a century, aptly described Rohit's batting, saying, 'Rohit batted really well. I think he did the same thing (V.V.S.) Laxman used to do, batting with the tailenders. He was 50-odd when we were eight down, and to score a century is a big achievement.' Pujara was obviously referring to the 280-run seventh-wicket partnership Rohit had crafted with R. Ashwin at the Eden Gardens. It was a new Indian record for that wicket.

Two centuries in his first two innings was a dream start to Rohit's journey. Here was a batsman who was branded a one-day specialist because of his tendency to play strokes from the first ball. It took him another 35 innings before he could hit his third century in Tests.

Kapil Dev, who has been a huge supporter of his style of batting, observed, 'I think it was a matter of concentration. He was seen to be playing loose shots that cost him his wicket. At the international stage, you have to value your wicket because the bowlers are out to get you. Rohit had built a strong reputation in one-day cricket and the splendid two-centuries start to his Test career meant he was the marked man. It was a combination of factors like high expectations and his sometimes-casual approach that saw Rohit not being able to keep up the early promise.'

Rohit was part of a run feast at Nagpur in the 2017 Test against Sri Lanka. Four home batsmen—Murali Vijay, Cheteshwar Pujara, Virat Kohli and Rohit—piled on the misery of the bowlers as Sri Lanka ran into four run-getters in great form. It was a relief for Rohit to have struck his third

Test century at a time when the critics were getting impatient with his failure to produce big innings. Scoring a century at number six when three of the preceding batsmen had crossed the 100-mark needed Rohit to apply himself. 'It was a test of his temperament,' observed coach Dinesh Lad. Rohit passed the test with ease.

Having secured his place in the Test team, it was imperative for Rohit to make the most of his good form. Some believed that having opened the innings in ODIs, he was also suited to perform the role in Tests, but he did not receive any opportunities. He had to struggle to command a regular place in the Test team, getting to play only 32 Tests even as Kohli played 68 Tests during that period.

Rohit played five Tests in 2014 when India played a total of 10. This was slow progress for him. His best year was 2015, when he figured in seven of the nine Tests that India played, but only three half-centuries in 13 innings did not quite endear him to the think tank of the team. The captain expected better and bigger contributions from Rohit, who had been nurtured as the key figure in the middle order. He fared slightly better in 2016, when he had three half-centuries in seven innings. India played 12 Tests that year, and Rohit was not able to win a consistent slot for himself.

Hans observed, 'I think it was a make-or-break stage for Rohit. He had to produce the big innings that we had come to expect from him. He was excelling in domestic cricket and the ODIs but had to translate the good form into runs in Test matches. That is where you make the difference. The decisive step comes when you excel on the big stage and Rohit was undoubtedly trying his best. You also have to consider the luck factor. There are times when you are concentrating but a good delivery can bring an end to your plans. I never had any doubts that Rohit was a classy player and was set to do well as a Test player.'

The year 2017 was very challenging for Rohit. Only two Tests came his way even as India played in 11 Tests against Bangladesh, Australia and Sri Lanka. Rohit felt the pressure from his critics and his self-proclaimed goals seemed to be slipping away. He hardly succeeded in regaining his form in 2018.

Rohit figured in four Tests, all overseas, in 2018—two each against South Africa and Australia. The South African stint was part of a losing experience as India came a cropper against pace at Cape Town and Centurion. The South Africans had done their homework and employed the quartet of Vernon Philander, Dale Steyn, Morne Morkel and Kagiso Rabada. It was a relentless assault, rekindling memories of the West Indian tactics of the 80s and 90s when speed was used to rattle the opposition. India lost all 20 wickets at Cape Town to fast bowlers. Once again, questions were raised regarding its batsmen's ability to perform overseas.

It was a poor experience for Rohit as he came up with scores of 11 and 10. To the chagrin of its fans, the Indian team failed to score 208 runs to win and collapsed for a miserable 135 as its batting stood exposed. It would have been worse but for a swashbuckling 93 by Hardik Pandya in the first innings, the result of a desperate attempt where Pandya threw his bat at everything that came his way.

It was no different in the next Test as India travelled to Centurion, the ground where the Indian fans had some great memories of the 2003 World Cup win against Pakistan. Rohit contributed 10 in the first innings and redeemed some of his prestige with 47 in the second innings, emerging the highest scorer, although India failed to reach the target of 287 by 135 runs. This was disappointing for Rohit, as this was a chance to cement a place in the middle order. India lost the series 2–1 and with it the claims of being a good travelling unit. The overseas loss caused a big dent in the team's reputation.

Rohit missed the two-Test series at home when Prithvi Shaw made a dramatic entry into the world of cricket. An excellent product of the Mumbai school of cricket, Shaw emulated Rohit by cracking a century in his Test debut, scoring 134 at Rajkot and laying the base for India's comprehensive victory. India wrapped up the series in the next match in Hyderabad. All eyes were on the tour to Australia, for this was going to be an acid test. Rohit was among those who left the country with high hopes of winning the series.

The four-match series was promoted as the clash between the best two best-playing nations in the world. India was looking to win its first ever series in Australia, and as coach Ravi Shastri had claimed, the team had the potential to do it. Kohli was more than confident because India had the attack to take 20 wickets. 'Bowlers win you matches,' was always Kapil Dev's opinion. And he was proved right on this tour.

Six members of the team—Virat Kohli, Cheteshwar Pujara, Ajinkya Rahane, Rishabh Pant, Mohammed Shami and Jasprit Bumrah—played all the four matches. Pujara emerged the pillar of India's batting with three centuries and a tour aggregate of 521 runs. He was the decisive factor in the win. Kohli and Pant got a century each, but again Rohit did not rise to the occasion. His four innings fetched him a mere 106 runs. This rankled

Rohit, as his future as a batsman in Tests seemed uncertain. He had failed to translate his opportunities into a chance to carve a permanent place in the middle order. He had again got out after making a good start.

Nevertheless, Rohit was a part of the history-making team, which won its first-ever series in Australia with a 2–1 margin. India's win came in the first Test (Adelaide) and the last (Melbourne), with a loss at Perth and a drawn encounter at Sydney.

Rohit's contribution in the win at Adelaide was 37 and 1, but more importantly, he played a role in the win, which gave the team much-needed confidence. A setback in the form of a loss at Perth saw the series tied at 1–1, but Rohit missed this match on account of a back injury. When he returned to the playing XI for the third Test at Melbourne, he brought luck with him and produced a gritty 63 not out in the first innings as India established early control. Then Bumrah dealt Australia three crucial blows in the second innings, setting up a famous victory. India was on course to clinch the series. A draw at Sydney, which Rohit had to forego due to paternity leave, brought unprecedented joy and praise for this brave bunch of cricketers who were making history. Rohit was a proud member of the side.

He did not figure in the two-match Test series in the West Indies in 2019. In the absence of seam bowler Hardik Pandya, Kohli preferred to play Hanuma Vihari, who also offered off-spin bowling options. Vihari won the toss-up between him and Rohit only because he could bolster the bowling. Kohli said on the eve of the Test, 'Vihari gives you a few overs with the ball as well. He's a solid player. Rohit, we've been seeing it for years, so it's about who provides the best balance in terms of the XI we want to choose. Rohit's also done well in Melbourne (the previous tour). It all depends on the kind of combination we want to go with.It was a terrible time for Rohit to sit out despite being in the best form of his career. He had led India's campaign at the World Cup in England with a record five centuries. Vihari had prepared for the series with the India "A" team, and he and Rohit were among the runs in the tour match in Coolidge. It was doubtless a tough choice for Kohli, but it was extremely harsh as far as Rohit was concerned. It was hardly surprising that India steamrolled the West Indies. But Rohit was back in the reckoning for the home matches against South Africa and Bangladesh.'

Critics were mighty pleased with Rohit finally playing to his potential against South Africa, displaying the authority that he has been associated with and scoring a century in each innings as the South Africans were hit hard in the opening Test at Visakhapatnam. Openers Mayank Agarwal and Rohit came up with a resounding partnership of 317 runs to make the South Africans grovel. Agarwal smashed 215 and Rohit a fluent 176. This was India's latest opening pair, and Rohit eased into the responsibility in his first innings as a Test opener. He was tested, as was Agarwal, by speedsters Rabada and Philander, but South Africa had run into a solid wall. Rohit and Agarwal were locked in a competition to outdo each other, and that was bad news for the bowlers.

Even though Agarwal made an impression on the spectators, it was Rohit's effortless innings that left them in a trance. The ease with which he got into position to play his strokes confirmed his calibre. His second visit to the crease was equally entertaining as he reached a scintillating 127. This was one of the finest knocks of his career. Rohit said, 'The talk was on for a long time about me opening the innings. In the West Indies they told me clearly that it's going to happen now. So mentally I was ready for it. Opening the batting in red-ball cricket is a different ball game compared to limited overs. You have to train your mind more than anything else. Technically, yes, you have got to look into it, certain aspects of batting. I was clear on what I wanted to do. There was no confusion in my mind. When you are playing international cricket, you always look for opportunities. Yes, there will be a lot of challenges ahead but I'm not focusing on all of those. It's pretty important for me to stay in the present and think about what I need to do today. I was very clear in my mind. The initial period will be tough. You have to focus on the basics. Playing close to your body, leaving the ball. In India, after the early overs, the ball doesn't swing.'

He was thrilled to be declared the 'Man of the Match'.

The next outing at Pune was quite forgettable for Rohit, but what followed at Ranchi was a defining moment for the Mumbaikar. His maiden double century could not have come at a better point in his career. That he won his second successive 'Man of the Match' award was hardly surprising. He had been hurt by the experience of sitting out in the West Indies and was now going to grab every little chance that came his way to establish his claims as a Test batsman. Getting to open the innings was the best thing to happen to his game since he was performing the role to perfection in ODIs. He only had to come up with a few adjustments to his style when batting in a Test match.

His 212 was a package of entertainment, almost a series of highlights, for he blasted 28 fours and six sixes. 'It was more of an ODI knock,' noted former all-rounder Madan Lal, who was always a supporter of Rohit as a stroke player in all formats of the game. 'If you are good in Tests, you can innovate in the other two formats too, and Rohit is one batsman who has all the shots in his book and is best suited to dominate.'

The critics caught some interesting statistics. His first three centuries in Tests came over four years but the next three in merely 18 days. The South Africans discovered his potential the hard way. Speaking at the end of the first day's play at Ranchi, the Indian team's batting coach, Vikram Rathour, praised Rohit saying, 'I always believed that he was too good a player to not be playing in any format. It was a good call to make him open. And with the amount of runs he has scored, he has settled the issue for the time being. With the kind of experience he has, if he starts coming good at the top of the order, that changes everything for the team, even when we are touring.'

Rathour was pleased with how Rohit had handled the hostile Kagiso Rabada. 'That's what Test cricket is all about. Rabada showed why he is rated so highly. There was movement for him. Good batsmen should survive those spells and stay in the middle and Rohit did that well. And once you start bowling to his strength, he will punish you,' he said.

Had Rohit worked on his technique ahead of the series, Rathour was asked. 'I don't think he needed to change his technique,' he said. 'He just had to make that mental adjustment. Once he is set, he is a phenomenal player.' The conditions were hostile and according to Rathour, Rohit responded well. 'Rohit needed to survive that early period, and if he looked uncomfortable doing that, it's because anybody will. Those were tough conditions. But once the wicket settled down, he batted really well,' said the batting coach.

It was pretty clear that he was enjoying his newfound status in the team. Rohit was candid when he reflected on his two Tests against South Africa. At the press conference after his double century, he said, 'It's not like only after opening I wanted to do well. Wherever I used to play even before, I always tried to do well. Right now, I've played only three Test matches as an opener, so there's a long way to go. I'm not reading too much into it but, of course, I'll take a lot of positives from it. Opening the batting is a different challenge compared to batting at six or five or seven. Because playing the first ball of a match, compared to playing after 30–40 overs, it's a different ball-game. You have to be mindful of which ball you have to play at and which ball you have to leave. I was allowing myself to take time, rather than going after the bowlers straightaway. You also have to play with a low backlift and things like that, in these conditions.'

When Rohit went for lunch at 199, he was asked how he coped with the tension. He said with good humour, 'I wouldn't say it's frustrating. It's just the laws of the game. The time it has to finish, it has to finish. I was not thinking about (the 200) at all. I knew that whenever it's supposed to happen, it will happen. In terms of what was thrown at me in this particular Test match, I would definitely say that this was probably the most challenging knock. I had to use this opportunity fully, otherwise I knew you guys would write a lot about me. But now you can write something good.'

The innings had done wonders to his mood, his career and place in the team.

Rohit concluded 2019 on a disappointing note though—knocks of 6 and 21 against Bangladesh in the two-match series at Indore and Kolkata. He was hardly perturbed. He was not going to worry about his place in the Test team anymore. He was batting at his preferred slot. And he was shaping up fine to look at a prosperous career in the longest format of the game.

TWO

Through the Eyes of His Coach

Cricketers are born and not made. This is what the man who gave Indian and world cricket Rohit Sharma believes. He has imbibed this principle from his guru 'Dronacharya' Ramakant Achrekar.

Dinesh Lad, who played cricket for his employers Western Railway, has made huge strides in cricket coaching. He has guided the careers of more than 80 cricketers who have played representative cricket with reasonable success, their levels varying from age-group for the state to the highest level one can only dream about, and all the levels in between.

Rohit is undoubtedly the biggest player Lad has produced. He has also produced Mumbai's gutsy Ranji Trophy batsman Siddhesh Lad, his son, as well as India's limited overs pacer Shardul Thakur, even providing shelter at his home in Borivali as the pacer hailed from distant Palghar and travelling daily for cricket was not possible.

Rohit faced a similar problem when seeking admission at Borivali Sports and Cultural Association (BSCA) as a 12-year-old. He had to move in to his uncle's (father's brother) residence in the western suburb of Mumbai while his parents continued to stay in the distant central suburb of Dombivli.

Lad liked the sight of Rohit bowling off-spinners the first time he saw the youngster. It was in a summer tournament between Lad's Swami Vivekananda International School (SVIS) and the BSCA, for which Rohit was turning out.

Lad recalls the year 1999, when he came across the young off-spinner who went on to become the 'Hitman' that bowlers the world over dreaded in later years.

'In 1999, I saw Rohit while playing a match against us. As there are so many coaching camps going on in April–May, Borivali Sports and Cultural Association too was conducting a camp. Rohit was staying near the ground with his uncle. He wanted to join the club for the one-and-a-half-month summer camp, the fee for which was Rs 800.00.

'Rohit joined them. They organised three–four tournaments for U-10, 12, 14, 16. My school team (Swami Vivekananda) also participated in the tournament and reached the U-12 final against Rohit's BSCA. It was a 10-over match on a cement pitch. They scored 67 runs. I don't remember how he batted but when his team bowled, Rohit sent down two overs. I was very impressed the way he bowled.'

Rohit continued to only bowl in Lad's nets and did not get to bat until a year later. It is Lad's coaching style to give only bowling to his bowlers in the nets and batting only to batsmen.

The 59-year-old Lad reminisces, 'I was trying to build a cricket team for the school that started in 1995. I was appealing to parents to enrol their wards in Swami Vivekananda International School. After that particular final, I approached Rohit and asked to meet his parents. He said his parents did not live in Borivali and that he was staying with his uncle. I met his uncle, who came to watch the match, and told him his nephew was very good. I told him if he wanted to change the school, he could come to Swami Vivekananda School two days later.'

On the appointed day of 2 June 1999, Rohit's uncle met Lad at the school and was taken to the school director, Yogesh Patel. Lad remembers that day vividly, 'I took the admission form for Rohit and told the school director that I wanted to get Rohit admitted in the school. He immediately cleared the form. His uncle asked me what the fees was. It was Rs 275 per month for Class 7. His uncle immediately asked for withdrawal of the admission form as he said he could not afford to pay that much. He said the school Rohit was currently going to collected a fee of Rs 30 per month. I said to his uncle, "The school was doing admission without any donation, the school was good and Rohit would get to play."'

Rohit's uncle explained to Lad the financial difficulties they faced before admitting him into BSCA. Lad quoted Rohit's uncle: 'To get Rohit admitted into the club to play cricket, we five brothers have contributed Rs 50 each, and collected remaining fees from friends here and there.'

Rohit came to SVIS from a humble background with his father working in a transport company. Lad recalls, 'Rohit's father was working in a transport company for a meagre salary and staying at Dombivli with wife and younger son. Rohit was staying with uncle in a small house with three families and his grandmother (father's mother) in Borivali.'

Lad went back to the school director with the admission form and told him the situation Rohit was in. Lad said, 'I requested him to waive the fees for Rohit. He became the first student of the school to be given freeship. I told the director that Rohit came from a poor background and could not afford the fees, and that the boy was talented in cricket.

'He immediately agreed to give Rohit freeship. If not for the freeship that the director agreed to give Rohit, we would not have seen Rohit the cricketer that he is today. Having been granted freeship, his family agreed to get him admitted in the school, and the rest is history.'

Mumbai schools have two tournaments annually for schools—Harris Shield for U-16 and Giles Shield for U-14. Like his illustrious seniors Sachin Tendulkar and Vinod Kambli, who made Harris Shield world famous with their 664-run stand in 1988, or those who came after him like Sarfaraz Khan (439 in Harris Shield in 2009), Armaan Jaffer (498 in Giles Shield in 2010) and Prithvi Shaw (546 in Harris Shield in 2013), Rohit too came up from these tournaments.

Although Rohit did not set fire to these tournaments with triple and quadruple centuries like some other players have, he was consistent with the bat and ball from his second year. He also took a hat-trick in one of the school matches. He would recall this feat after a match at Centurion in South Africa in the second edition of the IPL in 2009, where he took a hat-trick for Deccan Chargers against Mumbai Indians. Lad also remembers Rohit's hat-trick in that school game. 'Rohit was in his second last year in school. Siddhesh was 10 years. Siddhesh played in that game and scored 40-odd while Rohit got out early. But, when it came to bowling, Rohit took seven wickets including a hat-trick in that match.'

It was only in his second year at SVIS that Rohit got to bat. Lad looked at Rohit's talent as a spinner but did not predict that he was team India material straightaway, as some coaches shoot their mouths after looking at a young talent. Lad says, 'I was not looking far ahead in that Rohit would go on to play for the country. I only looked at the talent, the way he bowled. I was very impressed with the way he bowled with a superb, natural action. He gave away only three runs and took one or two wickets in that final. I was so impressed that I wanted him in my school.'

'Those days, we started practice in school in October for U-16. Rohit was only 12 then. After Harris Shield ended, we started practice for Giles Shield. Rohit was regular for practice. However, that year, we lost in the early rounds of Giles Shield. Rohit had to wait for the next academic year to make a mark for himself in the school tournaments.'

Though he was only 13, Lad took him in the Harris Shield team. Lad says, 'The way he bowled in those matches in his first year, I took him in Harris Shield team when he was only 13 and in Class 8. There were other talented 12 and 13-year-olds who were also fielded in Harris Shield. One day, while I was entering the school gate, I noticed a boy taking knocks at the nets and was hitting neatly from the middle of the bat. Initially, I could not recognise him. The way he knocked the ball, I was very impressed. I called for him and asked, "Rohit, can you also bat?" He replied shyly, "Yes, sir."

'The kid was afraid to say that to me. I asked him, "Batting *karega*?" ("Will you bat?") He said, "*Haan karoonga*." ("Yes, will do.") I told him to open the batting in the nets. He said he felt like he was floating in the sky with joy of being asked to bat because after one year, he was getting to bat. The way he batted, I was very pleased.'

Rohit, the opening batsman, was born that day. 'I sent Rohit to open in Giles Shield. He scored 140-plus in his first match as an opener. There was no looking back from then.'

Lad's coaching methods include not interfering with a player's technique but only fine-tuning here and there and retaining the individual's style of play. Lad says, 'I never say I prepared Rohit. I only tell him things like, "Do this, do that." I believe that nobody can make a cricketer. A cricketer is born and not made. To me, a cricketer has talent. That talent has to be groomed. Of course, luck also is a major factor. You have to teach simple things, not complicate them. If he is a good learner, he will learn quickly. If he has talent and focuses on his game, he will make a good cricketer. People say to me, "You have made Rohit, you have made Shardul (Thakur), you have made Siddhesh. You are a very good coach." I tell them, "No, not at all. They are naturally talented, I only guided them with simple things."'

It was when Rohit went to Class 10 that his performances peaked. Rohit, the cricketer, arrived. He scored about a dozen centuries in all tournaments in that academic year, including the Harris Shield. It was then that Lad said, 'Rohit was going to play top-level cricket in the future, not necessarily for India.'

During the COVID-19 lockdown, Lad has restricted his coaching to his four-year-old grandson (daughter's son). Lad says the same thing about his grandson: 'He will go on to play top-level cricket in the future.'

As used to be the norm with state selectors then, they used to watch performances of schools from Churchgate up to Bandra, Lad reveals. 'They never went beyond Bandra and into the distant suburbs,' he says.

Thankfully for Lad, his friends and former Ranji Trophy players Sanjay Patil and Shankar More were in the junior selection panel.

'Sanjay Patil and Shankar More were Mumbai selectors and I knew them very well. I told Sanjay, "You watch only players from the town side, you should watch players from my area as well." Sanjay and Shankar soon came to my school and saw Rohit bat. They said "*Kya talent hai!*" ("What a talent!")'

Talented Rohit certainly was, and it was this talent that has taken him the world over, setting cricket grounds afire with his stylish strokes and powerful hits and fetching him 14,029 runs from 364 international appearances with 39 centuries and 74 half-centuries.

Rohit's joy knew no bounds when Lad presented him with a Gray Nicolls bat and a proper kit, all the more because of his humble background.

Lad remembers how that year went for Rohit.

'There was a tournament for U-14 teams called Samna Trophy, and teams from Pune, Vidarbha besides Mumbai "A" and "B" participated in it. Rohit was selected in one of the teams. As it was his first selection for an important tournament, I gave him a Gray Nicolls bat and a good pair of pads. I was very happy for him. But, he did not get to play in that tournament. He came back to me and cried that he was not given a chance to play. I asked the coach of his team why he was not selected, and was told that Rohit was unwell. Rohit denied that he was unwell and that he was fully fit.

'Next was the Kalpesh Koli tournament to select Mumbai probables, and he was selected for that too. However, he did not get to play in that too as he had to compete with another talented off-spinner and batsman and that player was given preference.'

It was not long before Rohit made the most of the Gray Nicolls bat presented to him by Lad. As luck would have it, Lad says, the Board of Control for Cricket in India changed the age-group format from U-14 to U-15 and U-16 to U-17. Lad said, 'So, Rohit was eligible to play in U-15 and played in the next year's Kalpesh Koli tournament. He scored consistently to be named player of the tournament and was straightaway picked among Mumbai probables. Reputed coach and former Ranji Trophy player Vasu Paranjape was coach of Mumbai U-17 then.'

The annual Shatkar Tournament went well for Rohit, and based on his performances, he was selected for the Mumbai U-17 squad. Lad narrates: 'In the West Zone tournament, Rohit was not picked in the 11 for the first three matches. I spoke with Paranjape sir and he said others were also playing good. He said he would give Rohit a chance.

'Against Baroda, he got a chance as one of the players was injured. He scored 120-odd batting in the middle-order. He never opened in Mumbai age-group level and usually batted at No. 5. The coach was impressed, the selectors were impressed. Mumbai qualified for knockouts. Rohit scored well. He was selected for West Zone U-17 camp.'

After the camp, Rohit was in Bengaluru playing inter-zonal matches. That was the start of the *guru–shishya* (teacher-pupil) relationship between Praveen Amre, former India batsman and Ranji Trophy-winning Mumbai coach, and Rohit.

Lad recalls that his good friend Amre saw Rohit bat in Bengaluru. 'In one match, he was playing against Praveen's Air

India and scored more than 130. Praveen was very happy. He took him in Air India on scholarship.'

It was around that time that Saurashtra's Cheteshwar Pujara was blossoming into a sturdy batsman. He would go on to take the No. 3 slot in Tests and share the dressing room with Rohit from the U-19 journey up to Test cricket till date.

Lad recalls, 'Amre was the junior selection committee chairman. Rohit was selected for junior Asia Cup. He was performing well in U-19 zonal matches, was selected for West Zone. Legendary Mumbai left-arm spinner of yesteryear, Padmakar Shivalkar was spin bowling coach at zonal camp. He once said that Rohit was very good and that I tell him to continue bowling. He also mentioned about another talented boy called Pujara.

'But, Rohit did not impress in the U-19 selection matches leading to the ICC U-19 World Cup to be held in Sri Lanka in early 2006. Praveen said Rohit was not performing in the selection matches but added that Rohit's talent was so good that he could not be left out of the World Cup squad. Other national selectors did not concur with Praveen. But, Praveen had his way and picked Rohit for the World Cup. It was only because of Praveen that Rohit was selected for U-19 World Cup as he knew his batting very well.'

India finished second to Pakistan in that 2006 U-19 World Cup final. Rohit's performances in that tournament were not bad. With an aggregate of 205 runs in six innings (six matches) with three fifties and an average of 41.00, Rohit finished third among India's highest-run getters behind Pujara (349 at 116.33) and Karnataka's Gaurav Dhiman (222 at 44.40). Rohit's scores were 10 not out versus Namibia, 4 versus Scotland, 78 versus Sri

Lanka, 50 versus West Indies, 59 versus England in the semi-final and 4 against Pakistan in the final. Except against Scotland, when he opened the batting, Rohit batted at No. 3 throughout the entire tournament.

Such has been the turn of events since then that Rohit is among the most dangerous batsmen in limited overs cricket today with a world-record three double centuries in ODIs while Pujara has turned out to be one of the finest Test batsmen with not much success in the limited overs format for the country.

It is no secret that Rohit loves to hit sixes. Rohit's Mumbai team-mate Abhishek Nayar and his India U-19 captain and senior India team-mate Manoj Tiwary have spoken highly about Rohit's six-hitting abilities and how he hit fours and sixes with ease and at will. Rohit developed this ability at his school cement pitch with Lad throwing the ball from 16 yards.

Lad recounts this journey: 'Rohit's six-hitting abilities came natural to him. When he came to Class 10, at 15 years, he was batting beautifully with a straight bat. When selected for Mumbai team for T20 at 19, he once hit a six that sailed to the roof of Mumbai's Brabourne Stadium.'

There was no doubt about Rohit's talent, but Lad was particular about his focus on the game. Rohit had tasted success on the international stage at the U-19 level, so Lad's focus was on encouraging his ward to give more time to his game in the early stages of his career. 'He knew he wanted to be a cricketer, he did not know to do anything else,' Lad says.

'Every time I'd tell him, "Rohit, you have cricket, that's why people know you. If you are not disciplined, then you cannot move forward." I have seen many cricketers who were not successful because they were not focussed on their game.

You have to think about cricket. He has always been a good listener. He knew very well his family's financial position, where he came from. I tell him, "If you play well, you will get a job." He thought, "If I can play good cricket, I will get good job and raise money for the family." He was disciplined towards cricket. He used to bunk classes, tell the school principal that he had to go for practice. For five-six years, we used to practice daily. The school had a cement pitch. I used to throw a new ball at him from 16 yards, and he used to pull and square cut. The ball comes with even pace from a cement pitch. That's where he developed that cut and pull that became his key strokes. He had that talent.'

While Lad admits that Rohit did not stay with him, he spent a lot of time at his house and stayed close to him. 'Every day he used to come to my house from school and we'd go to practice daily.'

Rohit has, at every available opportunity, acknowledged Lad's role in shaping his career, saying it was because of his coach that he became a batsman from a bowler.

While Rohit gradually made his way into the Indian limited overs side shortly after turning 20, he had to wait for six years before making his Test debut, a format in which he is still finding his way. Late in 2019, he made his arrival as a Test opener with big centuries against South Africa.

Lad always believed that Rohit was ideal for all the three formats, but like most cricket followers believed, he felt Rohit threw away his wicket in Tests, showing his limited overs instincts when well set at the crease.

Lad says, 'I thought he was a perfect batsman for all the formats. The way he batted, be it in T20 or one-day, he hit the ball with straight bat. I thought he was good for Test cricket. But in Tests, he did not try to stay at the crease. Most of the time, he got out to spinners trying to hit him for a six. There is a lot of difference between hitting a white ball and red ball. White ball doesn't spin much whereas the red ball does. You cannot hit the ball properly.'

Before the Bangladesh tour selection, Lad and Rohit were sitting at school. Everyone knew Rohit was going to be selected for India.

After returning from the U-19 World Cup, Rohit made his List 'A' debut, representing West Zone in the Deodhar Trophy in the same month. In his debut against Central Zone, the same match in which the Saurashtra duo of Pujara and Ravindra Jadeja made their List 'A' debuts, Rohit scored an unbeaten 31 at No. 8 in a winning cause. In only his second List 'A' match, he scored an unbeaten 142 batting at No. 3 to lead a successful run chase against North Zone, pursuing a target of 278 in Udaipur. His 123-ball knock was laced with fourteen fours and three sixes.

While Rohit was knocking on the doors of international cricket, he had to wait until mid-2007 when he was picked for the tour of United Kingdom, where he made his ODI debut under Rahul Dravid's captaincy against Ireland in Belfast, not getting to bat at all.

Rohit was upset in the months preceding the UK tour, when he was expecting to be picked for the Bangladesh tour. Lad revisits that period, saying, 'He was not originally picked for Bangladesh tour while Punjab's Dinesh Mongia was preferred. Rohit was very upset. I told him, he was only 20 and that he had to keep performing, not to take tension and that his chance would come. He regularly practiced. His mantra would be, "Sir, practice *karna hain*" ("want to practice").'

It was that Bangladesh tour where Manoj Tiwary was injured just when he was on the cusp of his India debut, and it was Rohit's turn to take his place in the UK tour that followed.

While Rohit did not get any game to play in the ODIs against England, he was on the flight to South Africa for the 2007 World T20 under Mahendra Singh Dhoni.

Rohit missed the first three matches, not getting to bat in his debut against England. But he made an impression straightaway when he scored an unbeaten 50 against South Africa in his second T20I appearance in Durban, bagging the 'Man of the Match' award. Rohit also played a crucial hand of 30 not out in India's five-run win against Pakistan in the final to lift the inaugural World T20 title.

In the occasions that he was not initially selected in the playing XI in the World T20 in South Africa, Rohit would call his coach Lad daily. Lad recounts, "*Pakk gaya, yaar*" ("I am frustrated, sir"). His standard phrase was "*Pakk gaya*" ("I am frustrated"). I said to him, "Are you mad or what? You are in the Indian team, not any gully cricket team." He used to say whenever he got a chance, he would make it big and make it count. I advised him to be patient and that whenever he got a chance, he would do well. He did get to bat against South Africa and besides scoring 50 not out, effected a run out to dismiss Justin Kemp with a pick up and throw direct into the stumps.'

It was a triumph not only for the Indian team but also for Lad, who was hounded by media-persons into the wee hours of the next day. While the whole nation was celebrating India's success and the team was given a grand welcome from Mumbai airport to the Wankhede with the fans lining up the streets cheering the cricketers, Rohit treated himself to eggs after the felicitations at Lad's house.

Rohit loves eggs. And since he hails from an orthodox Brahmin family, even eggs are a strict no-no in his household. Rohit used to ask Lad to prepare eggs at his house for him. This was a regular practice at Lad's since Rohit was 12. Lad recalls fondly: 'After 2007 World T20 triumphant team was felicitated in Mumbai, Rohit said to me he was hungry and wanted to come home. I asked what he wanted. He said, *"Anda khana hain"* ("Want to eat eggs"). He and a couple of friends including my son Siddhesh consumed 65 eggs that evening.'

Another thing that Rohit is fond of is cars. Lad says that even as Rohit's parents moved in from Dombivli to Borivali and rented a place in the same building as Lad, the cricketer's mind was on buying a car and not owning a house.

Lad recollects, 'One day he came to me and said, "Sir, *bahut tension mein hoon*" ("I am tensed"). He was going for U-19 World Cup. I asked him what happened. He said, *"Papa ka job nahin, bahut tension mein hain"* ("My father does not have a job. I am tensed"). I called his father and told him not to give tension to Rohit but to call me directly for anything. I have never seen his father except once as he would never come to his matches. I told him not to take tension. I took a rental place in my building. I had Rs 60,000 in my Provident Fund account. I took Rs 50,000 from that and gave it as a deposit for the house in my building. His parents moved into my building. I also talked to my friend in Indian Oil Rajesh Jadhav to recruit Rohit.'

Till date, Rohit has been part of the Indian Oil Corporation family, which also has Wasim Jaffer, Cheteshwar Pujara, Ajinkya Rahane among other cricketers in its ranks.

The year 2008 saw the arrival of the Indian Premier League and Rohit, then the future of Indian cricket, was acquired by Deccan Chargers for USD 7.50 lakh (then approx. Rs 3 crore). He had already begun to see more money through his exploits with the bat.

Lad says, 'After CB series win in Australia just before the inaugural IPL, BCCI gave each player a bonus. Rohit booked a Skoda car. His father was angry about it. Rohit called and told me to make his father understand. He said everyone from his team including Sreesanth, Harbhajan Singh and a few others had booked a car with the winnings. I asked him, "Are you mad, why spend on a luxury car?" He said, "Leave it, sir." I told his father to let his son do what he wished, not to take tension. His parents are simple as they have not seen this much money, so they value money.'

Recounting another incident about Rohit's fondness for cars, Lad said, 'One day, we were standing on the road. He had just returned from the U-19 World Cup. There came a new top-end car parked next to us. He told me, "Sir, one day, I will buy this kind of a car. I used to call him, *"Pagal hain kya?"* ("Are you mad?")'

Rohit was so much into cars that one day he called Lad and said he would go out and be back in a while. Lad recalls: 'I asked him where he was going. He was going to take a Skoda car. I said, "Are you mad or what? When buying a house is a priority, why think of a car now?" But, that's Rohit for you.'

With his bank balance rising, Rohit eventually bought a house in Bandra, much against Lad's wishes.

'He got a house in Bandra as he said it was easy for him to go to practice at Bandra-Kurla Complex from there. He said, "Why take tension for this, allow me to buy a house in Bandra, *na*." He moved to Bandra alone, his parents continued to stay in my building.'

Lad attributes Rohit's dip in performances in 2009 and 2010 to his shifting base to Bandra all alone, living with friends. This eventually led to him not finding a place in India's triumphant 2011 World Cup campaign, a regret that Rohit carries till this day.

Lad too feels for Rohit.

'He got good chances in the build-up to that 2011 World Cup but did not score well. His performances were so pathetic that at one stage, after back-to-back hundreds in Zimbabwe in 2010, he averaged only 18.125 in 16 innings leading up to the 2011 World Cup.'

'When the World Cup team was announced, Rohit was very upset. I called him over to my place and gave him a piece of my mind for about 30 minutes. As he was staying with friends alone in Bandra, he was not giving much time to his cricket. His focus was diverted. One of the national selectors said to me that Rohit would not be picked up for the World Cup as he did not have performances to back him.

'I told Rohit, "You are stuck going to Bandra." After 2007 World T20, he used to come regularly to me for practice. Every time he'd ask me to come early from work for practice. After shifting to Bandra, he was roaming there and rarely came to me. I told him even Virat Kohli, who came into the national side after him, has cemented his place in the national team. That day, he told me, "Sir, from today you would not get any complaint about me."'

Lad says that it's every cricketer's dream to play in a World Cup and win. While Rohit was very upset about not getting selected for the 2011 World Cup, he knew he had himself to blame for that.

But Rohit kept his word and practised vigorously at BKC, seeking inspiration from Sachin Tendulkar, whom Rohit looked up to as an idol like every other Indian.

Lad remembers one conversation with Rohit, who by this time had joined Mumbai Indians in the IPL and was under the wing of his idol Tendulkar.

Lad says, 'One day, Rohit called me and said, "Sir, Sachin *kitna practice karte hain*" ("how long he practices!"). I said to him, "You had to also do the same amount of practice."'

Inspired by Tendulkar and the Mumbai Indians captaincy from 2013, Rohit has never looked back. Much to the joy of Lad, Rohit has 27 ODI hundreds post the 2011 World Cup, including three double hundreds and four T20I hundreds. He made a century on his Test debut in November 2013. In all, 37 of his 39 international centuries have come after that 2011 World Cup selection disappointment. Lad regards this as one of the turning points in Rohit's career. Not being picked for the 2011 World Cup has made Rohit reassess his career and put it back on the right track.

Though Rohit played significant knocks in the subsequent World Cups in 2015 and 2019, scoring a total of six centuries including five in the latest edition, the disappointment of not being a part of the winning team still hurts Rohit. Perhaps his dream of being a World Cup winner can be fulfilled in 2023 when the World Cup returns to India.

Rohit's captaincy for Mumbai Indians has won him many accolades. Lad said that leadership came naturally to Rohit from his school days.

'He had leadership qualities right from the school days, winning matches on his own, consistently taking three-four wickets and scoring hundreds. I gave him school captaincy in 2001 in Class 9. He was very aggressive, always wanted to win. That's what you play sport for, isn't it? That's the same with Rohit. He was only thinking of winning and himself contributing to it.'

Lad also lauds Rohit's self-confidence. Having seen him open the batting for his school, Lad was not surprised when he opened for India and scored those big hundreds.

'I always tell him to stay calm at the crease. As his technique is good, he just needs to stay in the crease and settle down. Once he does that, nobody can dislodge him. He has self-confidence and knows it very well,' Lad says.

THREE

The Grind of Domestic Cricket

Rohit's maiden first-class outing against New Zealand White at Darwin in 2006 laid the base for his steady progress. It was quite a competitive game against an opposition that included seamers Chris Martin and Hamish Bennett and spinners Jeetan Patel and Bruce Martin, all of whom went on to represent the senior national team in Tests later. Rohit was part of the India 'A' squad, which included players such as Cheteshwar Pujara, Shikhar Dhawan and S. Badrinath, who used the tour to strengthen their claims to the senior league. Rohit was obviously determined to grab this chance, and he did it in style with an innings of 57.

Recalling that knock, his teammate Reetinder Singh Sodhi observed, 'Rohit stood out with his excellent timing of the ball. He was always in the best of positions and seemed to have all the time in the world to play his shots. What we remembered most about him was the confidence that he carried to the middle. The innings was quite an indication that he was going to have a promising career. It was up to him how he used the platform. I am glad he launched his career on a very positive note.'

In the next outing, which was against Australia at Cairns, Rohit played a decent knock of 41. The Australian challenge was led by excellent players such as Phil Jaques, who cracked a double century, Shane Watson, Chris Rogers, Shaun Marsh, Brad Haddin, the incisive fast bowlers Mitchell Johnson and Shaun Tate. Middle-order batsman Y. Venugopal Rao recalled, 'Rohit looked set for a big innings when he fell to Watson. He made an impression on that tour.'

The tour was part of the process the Board had launched to give the youngsters a peep into the challenge of playing in Australia. The bouncy pitches and the fast bowlers were a different set-up for the Indians. Rohit had learnt his lessons well—he did not flinch. That was a good sign, since he was facing pace of that quality for the first time.

The national selectors were convinced of Rohit's talent, and he was picked for the West Zone team to play the Duleep Trophy even before he had turned out for Mumbai. In that match, he looked good in an innings of 41, the runs coming off bowlers such as S. Sreesanth and Anil Kumble. The highlight of the knock against South Zone was the range of shots that he displayed. Rohit, along with Ravindra Jadeja, faced Kumble with confidence even as his team collapsed against the wily leg-spinner.

Rohit's debut in Ranji Trophy came against Bengal at the iconic Eden Gardens in December 2006 with Amol Muzumdar at the helm of the Mumbai team. The home team dominated the contest, and Rohit saw from close quarters the importance of building an innings when Manoj Tiwary constructed an unbeaten 210. It was Tiwary's maiden century in first-class cricket, and it left a big impression on Rohit, who is now known for his aggressive batting. Rohit contributed a mere 21 in the middle order, but more importantly, he earned the Mumbai cap, which was just one rung below India colours.

Before the month ended, Rohit played in three more matches—against Punjab, Hyderabad and Gujarat. He was included in the first season, but there was pressure to justify his selection. He ensured that critics would not question his presence in the team with a crafty innings of 95 against Hyderabad. The knock prevented a win for Hyderabad even as Mumbai's disappointing run in the Ranji Trophy continued. It also led to a remarkable turning point in Rohit's career.

Rohit chose the Wankhede Stadium to make a strong statement as he decimated the Gujarat bowling to produce a double century, his first three-figure knock in first-class cricket. His 205 was a stroke-filled essay, and the range of his shots astounded his teammates. The knock also triggered a comeback for Mumbai, who won the match by an innings. The feat was repeated in the next match against Rajasthan at the same venue. Rohit enjoyed his stay in the middle with an innings of 72. He was batting with purpose, and the consistency was an aspect that impressed his teammates.

Rohit could get to bat only once, to make 30, as Mumbai crushed Maharashtra by an innings at Nasik. Three victories in a row was an amazing turn-around for Mumbai, which had conceded the first innings lead in its first three matches. In fact, Mumbai managed to avoid relegation from the Super League with three outright wins, followed by the astonishing win against Baroda in the semi-finals. This was Mumbai at its best. Scores of 6 and 0 against Baroda were lessons well learnt for Rohit. The final had Rohit experience the feeling of being part of a champion team as Mumbai won convincingly on home turf.

Bengal travelled to Mumbai with high hopes but ran into a determined Sachin Tendulkar, available for the final. Bengal was strengthened by the availability of Sourav Ganguly, but the honours belonged to Mumbai's players. The match saw Wasim Jaffer cross the 10,000-run mark in first-class cricket, Muzumdar enter the 5,000-run club and left-arm speedster Zaheer Khan make his debut for Mumbai after eight seasons with Baroda.

Rohit shared the dressing room with Tendulkar, watched him and Jaffer come up with centuries. He made his mark too after failing in the first innings. Promoted to bat at No. 3, Rohit hit a 57, the highest individual score for Mumbai in the second innings. His discipline in the middle saw Mumbai set up a daunting target of 472. Bengal made a spirited attempt through a strong middle-order response, but Mumbai proved unbeatable, the final margin of 132 runs aptly proving the difference between the teams.

The Ranji Trophy victory, 37th for Mumbai and first for Rohit, laid the foundation for his association with the game. Zaheer Khan's 5/40 and 4/119 had played a vital role, and the process was most pleasing for Rohit. To hold the Ranji Trophy in his hands was exactly the motivation he needed as his first season in first-class cricket had proved a rich experience.

Rohit's next outing was a short tour to Kenya and Zimbabwe, where he played three matches but failed to capitalise on a brilliant 66 he made in the first match against the home team at Harare. The experience of travelling with players such as Pujara, Parthiv Patel, Robin Uthappa, Mohammad Kaif, Irfan Pathan and S. Badrinath kept Rohit focussed on grabbing opportunities whenever they came his way.

His Ranji Trophy journey in 2007–2008 was restricted to five matches as Mumbai failed to progress beyond the league stage, beginning with a poor start against Delhi. In that match, they conceded the first innings lead on home turf. It was no different against Maharashtra, but a two-run victory against Rajasthan gave them a boost. Rohit's scores were 62 and 34. A draw against Himachal Pradesh hardly helped Mumbai, which fared below par against Saurashtra in a home game to bow out before the knockout stage. The Saurashtra match was a farewell contest for left-arm spinner Nilesh Kulkarni.

The 2008–2009 season began on an encouraging note for Rohit—a place in the Indian Board President's XI team for the tour match against the Australians in Hyderabad. Led by Ricky Ponting, the visiting team was keen to make the most of it at the start of the tour even as the local hopefuls sought to impress the national selectors. There was a healthy competition in the middle order, but Rohit won a slot in the playing XI.

The Board President's XI captain, Yuvraj Singh, summed up the situation well on the eve of the match: 'Even if you are not there, a strong performance will enhance your chances for there can be some changes anytime in the series. If I come up with a big score I don't see why I should not come back. And, to be a strong contender, you have to use this opportunity of playing against such a formidable Australian team. For me this is a chance to do well and stake my claim in the Test squad.'

The point was well taken by Rohit, who responded with a century that was to give him the confidence and push needed to play at the international level.

Yuvraj could not stake his claims in the first innings even as the top order of Aakash Chopra, Jaffer and Badrinath collapsed, leaving the stage for Rohit and a certain Virat Kohli to build their reputations. Rohit and Kohli produced identical scores of 105 in a fifth-wicket partnership of 146 runs against an attack consisting of Brett Lee, Mitchell Johnson, Stuart Clark and Peter Siddle.

Kohli loved the Rohit show from the other end of the pitch. Giving glimpses of his ability to pace the innings and come up with some stunning shots, Rohit picked Clark for special attention, playing the cut and pull off him with style, then slamming him over long-on for a six. It was a typical limited overs stroke but an essential part of Rohit's repertoire. He displayed his tendency to attack the bowlers by picking runs in a cascade off Jason Krejza, the off-spinner. True to his promise, Yuvraj signed off with a century on the last day.

Yuvraj did not get a look in against Australia in the four-Test series, which India won 2–0 to reclaim the Border–Gavaskar Trophy. The series was eventful since the legendary leg-spinner Anil Kumble took a bow from international cricket at the end of the third Test in Delhi. Kumble injured his left hand and needed 11 stitches, but he won the hearts of his fans with a farewell wicket—a running catch off his own bowling to dismiss Mitchell Johnson. Kumble finished with 619 Tests. What was to be the last ball of his career, a full toss, was hit for a four by Matthew Hayden.

Rohit returned to domestic cricket and did exceedingly well by aggregating 747 runs in seven matches (11 innings). The average of 74.70 placed him second in the team list, and three centuries showed him to be in consistent form. One century was against Rajasthan (128), and he closed the season with scores of

141 and 108 against Uttar Pradesh in Hyderabad as Mumbai won by 243 runs.

The start to the 2009–2010 season was sedate for Rohit with the Irani Cup against Rest of India in Nagpur. Mumbai's batting was blown away by the fast-bowling pair Munaf Patel (5/70), S. Sreesanth (3/46) and Sudeep Tyagi (2/56). Once they took the lead, Rest of India treated the second innings as batting practice to win the Cup for the fourth successive time.

It was a Ranji Trophy season to remember for Rohit, who finally played an innings that did justice to his stroke-making capacity and his endurance. After disappointing scores of 25 (against Punjab), 22 and 19 (against Himachal Pradesh), he warmed up with a fine 101 against Railways at the Karnail Singh Stadium in Delhi. He did not get to bat in the next match against Hyderabad but exploded with a magnificent 309 not out against Gujarat.

The audience at the Brabourne Stadium enjoyed his unbeaten 145 on the opening day. He told the Indian Express at the end of the day, 'There are several batsmen who score a hundred on a given day in Ranji cricket. I need to continue and score and a really big knock to stand out.' He kept his word when he resumed the next morning.

'After hitting the first ball for four I felt like I could continue to bat like yesterday,' he told the media after the day's play. 'The track was good and I knew it would be easier for me once Gujarat opts for the new ball. I just wanted to take it ball by ball. I was prepared to play my natural game even if I got out. But after crossing 200, I didn't want to take a chance.'

Rohit admitted that the knock was one of the finest in his career. He learnt a lesson in the next game against Haryana at

Lahli. Walking in at the fall of Wasim Jaffer's wicket to seamer Sachin Rana, he fell in the first delivery, casually driving the ball to cover. The Ranji Trophy season was over for Rohit even though Mumbai went on to win the title after a classic final against Karnataka at Mysore. He signed off the season with knocks of 63 and 116 against North Zone in the Duleep Trophy match at Rajkot. A significant milestone to take home from this match was crossing the 2,500-run mark.

Rohit played to his potential in the six matches of the 2010–2011 season even though Mumbai stumbled at the quarterfinal stage, losing to the eventual champion Rajasthan. It was Rajasthan's first-ever Ranji Trophy title after having finished runner-up on eight occasions between 1960–1961 and 1973–1974. Rohit topped the team's individual aggregate with 732 runs in 10 innings. The two centuries and four half-centuries he scored captured his consistency in a season of hope for him.

His centuries came against Bengal (200 not out) at the Eden Gardens and Delhi (148) at the Ferozeshah Kotla. He began on a rousing note with innings of 93 and 74 not out against Saurashtra, but Mumbai lacked the collective strength to make it to the summit fight. Rohit had come to establish himself as the batsman to watch as his reputation as a compulsive stroke player in all conditions grew.

Only three appearances in the 2011–2012 season saw Rohit garner 339 runs at an astonishing average of 113.00. The 175 against Railways set the tempo. 'It was tough but I enjoyed it,' he said after the innings. He followed it with a 100 against Rajasthan, which went on to retain the Ranji Trophy. In his final Ranji Trophy contest of the season, Rohit made 64 against Karnataka, which dominated the match with its batting might.

Rohit dominated the bowlers in the six matches that he played in the 2012–2013 season. An aggregate of 712 in ten innings showed his form and also the progress he made by putting value to his wicket: he cut out some of the flamboyance that made him throw away his wicket in the previous two seasons. This development did not go un-noticed, since Sachin Tendulkar acknowledged Rohit for his service to Mumbai cricket.

Rohit's scores were 18, 20 (vs Railways), 79 (vs Rajasthan), 112 (vs Hyderabad), 1, 14 (vs Bengal), 203, 28 (vs Punjab), 166, 71 (vs Saurashtra). In the innings against Rajasthan, Rohit crossed the 4,000-run mark in Ranji Trophy. The double century against Punjab at home was part of a run feast on a placid track. Punjab's Mandeep Singh hit a 211 to propel his team to an imposing total of 580, and Mumbai, thanks to Rohit's knock, made a spirited attempt but fell short by 95 runs. Mumbai's run culminated in a podium finish as it regained the Ranji Trophy with emphatic performances in the knockout stage with Tendulkar making himself available.

International commitments kept Rohit busy such that his next Ranji Trophy appearance was only in November 2015. Mumbai, led by Aditya Tare, played Uttar Pradesh at home. Rohit, in his 42nd Ranji Trophy match, contributed a splendid century (113). In the company of Shreyas Iyer (137), he out-batted Uttar Pradesh. Mumbai had developed a compact combination that carried the team to the title, the final against Saurashtra in Pune proving to be a one-sided match. The hectic schedule of the Indian team has not allowed Rohit to turn out for Mumbai since that century-show against Uttar Pradesh.

》》》》》

FOUR

Stepping into the Big League

It was so ironic. Geoff Boycott, who was dropped from the next Test for slow batting after scoring a double century, faced the first ball that heralded limited overs cricket. When he took guard against Australian speedster Graham McKenzie at the Melbourne Cricket Ground on 5 January 1971, he made history. It was the birth of a format that was to revolutionize the way cricket was played.

Over the years, limited overs cricket captured the imagination of its followers. It also helped sustain the game in terms of commercial returns from the matches. Its popularity rose to such an extent that administrators even came up with the inaugural World Cup in 1975, with the West Indies winning the tournament.

India took time to adapt to this demanding format. The emphasis was on combining endurance and agility. The epic triumph of 1983 when Kapil Dev's team won the title led to a huge fillip to the game in India. Hockey and football were completely overtaken, and cricket prospered to become the most popular game in India.

Rohit was not even born when India won that World Cup. But the game grew in stature with that amazing victory at Lord's such that it inspired a generation of youngsters to hope for a career in cricket. Among the millions who dreamt of cricketing glory was Rohit, who realized early in his life that his future lay in belting the ball.

The cricket culture of Mumbai, with its maidans beckoning aspirants, attracted Rohit to take to the game seriously. The legacy of the likes of Sunil Gavaskar and Sachin Tendulkar was rich, and he climbed the ladder with passion. Mumbai's reputation for producing awesome batting talent was reaffirmed by Rohit making it to the highest league.

With big scores in domestic cricket, Rohit proved to be on the right track as he earned a spot in the Indian team for two ODI matches in Ireland in June 2007. His debut against Ireland did not give him a chance to bat, and his score of 8 was disappointing. A one-off appearance in the ODI against Australia at Hyderabad in the same year saw Rohit fail to impress as he batted at No. 7 and manage just 1. In his next outing, against Pakistan at Jaipur, Rohit justified his inclusion with a brilliant 52, the top score of the India innings but not enough to stop Pakistan from winning comfortably. He earned praise from skipper M.S. Dhoni, who said, 'He was under pressure when he went out to bat. This was a match where guys, who sat out in the earlier matches, got an opportunity to play and that is important for the team.'

But the selectors kept that innings at Jaipur in mind. As a result, Rohit was picked for the Commonwealth Bank Series in Australia where he played in all the ten matches, one of seven Indians to figure in every contest. It was the first long run for the Mumbai batsman, and it gave him the stage he needed to cement his place. His response was an aggregate of 235 runs with two half-centuries. However, this was below expectations considering the faith Dhoni had in him.

The tournament saw Dhoni lead from the front even though Gautam Gambhir was in splendid form—440 runs with two centuries and a 50—and Tendulkar aggregated one run short of 400. The all-rounder strength of the team brought India the title when, drawing inspiration from some tremendous fast bowling by Ishant Sharma and Parveen Kumar, they prevailed upon Australia 2–0 in the finals. Rohit played a part in the first final with a fourth wicket association with Tendulkar, who came up with a scintillating 117 not out to fashion a thumping win. Tendulkar was the star again with 91 in the second final where Parveen claimed four wickets to win the 'Man of the Match' honours.

Rohit was part of a landmark feat—India's first ever triangular series in Australia. The youth element of Indian cricket made a sound statement in the most challenging circumstances against the world champions. The second final was clinched with just two balls remaining, and it showed the resolve of the young players to make history. India's previous title-winning show had come at the World Championship of Cricket in 1985 under Sunil Gavaskar's farewell tournament as skipper.

The chairman of the selection committee, Dilip Vengsarkar, called it 'a fantastic and historic victory'. He said, 'To defeat the top team over last one decade shows that India is fast closing in on Australia.' Navjot Singh Sidhu commented: 'It is definitely one of the top five wins recorded by India in its history. The lions have roared and they have announced their arrival. Indian cricket has a bright future.'

Former captain Ajit Wadekar also made a comment. 'It was a historic victory and reminded me of the 1971 (Test series) victories over the West Indies and England (away from home). It was a great team effort. Dhoni has led very well and the team is a nice blend of youth and experience. Sachin (Tendulkar) made a hell of a difference,' he said.

Rohit's ability to dictate terms in limited overs was not missed by the national selectors. He was an essential part of the Indian challenge when he was picked for the three-nation Kitply Cup at Dhaka involving Bangladesh and Pakistan. The Indians played their best in the league, winning both its matches, but faltered in the final, losing to Pakistan. Rohit's contributions were poor—9, 26 and 24.

There was more one-day cricket in store when India travelled to Sri Lanka to play five matches for the Asia Cup, held in Karachi. This was Rohit's next stop. Barring a 58 in the return match against Pakistan, he did little of note as India finished runner-up to Sri Lanka, losing the final by 100 runs. Rohit aggregated a miserable 72 in five innings, 32 his highest score, as India claimed the series 3–2, losing the first and the last match.

There was excitement among fans as England arrived for a seven-match ODI series. The last two matches at Guwahati and Delhi were unfortunately cancelled on account of the terrorist attack in Mumbai. India swept all the five matches but Rohit hit miserable form, aggregating 50 runs in four innings. It was a testing phase for him—the competition in the middle order had grown and he was yet to come up with a single compelling knock.

On the heels of the series against England, a three-match tour was squeezed in by India in Sri Lanka, with the home team losing 2–1. Rohit failed in all three visits to the crease. A 50 eluded him in the next seven matches as India played against New Zealand, the West Indies and South Africa. But there was joy in store when the team visited Zimbabwe for a tri-series, which Sri Lanka won.

It took Rohit 42 matches to cross the three-figure mark. He scored outstanding back-to-back ODI centuries against Zimbabwe (114) and Sri Lanka (101 not out) in the series. A sensational shot in that knock saw Rohit hitting left-arm spinner Ray Price out of the ground. His maiden century, however, went in vain as Zimbabwe won the match, in which three Indians—Umesh Yadav, R. Vinay Kumar and Ashok Dinda—made their debut. His century against Sri Lanka proved a match-winning effort.

Rohit became a part of the Asia Cup-winning team that tamed Sri Lanka in the final. His best was a 69 in a losing cause against Sri Lanka, but the 41 in the final was a crucial knock as it came in the latter half of the innings. His 50-run stand with Suresh Raina for the fifth wicket gave India a total to defend. A fine spell by left-arm fast Ashish Nehra prevented Sri Lanka from making it a hat-trick of Asia Cup titles. The tournament witnessed a classic when India beat Pakistan in the league—the win coming off the penultimate ball when Harbhajan Singh smashed Shoaib Akhtar for a six to close the acrimonious contest.

Rohit ran into a lean patch over the next seven matches that he played against New Zealand and South Africa. This cost him a place in the 2011 World Cup at home, and it hurt Rohit because he had looked forward to playing the prestigious tournament at home. He made no secret of his disappointment in various interviews, even though he was to play the 2015 and 2019 editions of the World Cup. The 2011 event at home was very special as India emerged the champion in the final at the Wankhede Stadium.

India's World Cup win at home was a celebration of the youth even though the team dedicated the win to Tendulkar's long-cherished dream of winning the Cup. Tendulkar played the most critical part with a game-winning knock in the tense semi-final against Pakistan at Mohali, a match watched by top dignitaries from the two nations. The tournament was a tribute to the collective efforts of the young brigade where batsmen played their part well, especially M.S. Dhoni, Virender Sehwag, Gautam Gambhir and Virat Kohli. The star of the tournament was Yuvraj Singh, who battled a life-threatening ailment to contribute handsomely to India's triumph. Yuvraj emerged the Man of the Tournament, aggregating 362 runs and his haul of 15 wickets second only to the 21 by Zaheer Khan.

After the 2011 World Cup, Rohit worked on his consistency and vowed not to gift his wicket to the opponents following criticism that he had begun to take his place for granted. There was some truth in the argument, but it was always going to be a tough task for Rohit because his shot selection was a matter of debate.

India all-rounder Manoj Prabhakar said, 'I felt for Rohit for the simple reason that he often batted under pressure when holding the fort in the middle order. When you open the innings, you get the best of everything. The ball is hard and the field restrictions of two fielders outside the circle help you plunder runs. I always thought he had a wide range of shots to beat any field and he did prove us right on many occasions. There were times when a good ball would consume his wicket or an excellent catch ended his promising knock. But there was no doubt that he was a very strong contender to grab the opener's slot.'

Prabhakar's observation was spot on. The opener's position came Rohit's way in the home series against England in 2012–2013. He was elevated to open the innings in the fourth match of the series at Mohali, and he celebrated the promotion with a knock of 83 that set up India's win. Raina's 89 gave the finishing touches, but the match was important for Rohit assuming the mantle of an opener, a slot he was not going to surrender.

The Mohali match also brought Rohit glowing praise from Dhoni. 'Where are the British journalists? Call them for the press conference now. They are usually there to add spice...' remarked Dhoni as he met the media after the match.

'I am very happy for Rohit. We all know he is a god-gifted talent. We had a discussion a few days ago and I am happy he took the challenge (of opening the innings). I think he can be a good opener because he cuts and pulls really well. Also, it is good to have one opener slightly more aggressive than the other. It is important to give some players a bit of rope, another chance, since we do not play too many ODIs after this series. Rohit went through a lean patch in Sri Lanka. At present, he cannot get into the squad in the middle-order. So this was the only opportunity for him to play for India.'

The series was to prove a remarkable turnaround in Rohit's one-day career. He had aspired to grab the spot vacated by Tendulkar in the previous season as the master batsman concentrated on extending his Test career to the 200-mark. The responsibility of opening the innings helped Rohit grow as a batsman, giving the innings a definite direction with his breathtaking range of strokes. The fact was that he became far more consistent once he realized his place was not under threat. He was assured of a long run, and that gave him the confidence he needed for a successful career in limited overs cricket. He had lost the chance of opening the innings following his miserable scores of 23, 1 and 5 in the ODI series in South Africa in the run-up to the 2011 World Cup.

It was his 18th innings as opener when Rohit exploded on the colourful arena at the Sawai Man Singh Stadium in Jaipur in 2013. His astonishing display of powerful shots often caused despair in the opposition as bowlers suffered even when they bowled tight. It was just that Rohit connected whatever he attempted that wonderful night as India chased down a stiff target of 360 runs.

He raced from 100 to 200 in a mere 42 balls. It was carnage as Australian bowlers were made to look mediocre by Rohit, who hit the ball at will. His 209 off 158 balls was peppered with 12 fours and 16 sixes. He took a huge step as a batsman of quality with this breathtaking performance. The stroke play was silken and at times brutal, but it was entertainment at its best. It was obvious that Rohit had utilized his experience from the IPL to pulverize the bowlers.

He was delighted at the record he set for the number of sixes in an innings. 'The goal was to get as many runs as possible. I really didn't know how many sixes I had hit. We won the series; that was the most heartening thing. Today was an ideal innings; I waited for an opportunity to play shots and it came out well.'

Rohit was candid in observing that he was aiming to score big. 'When I was batting, I didn't think about scoring 200 at all. The only thing on my mind was scoring big. When I got close to 183, then I felt it was possible. But I wasn't playing for the 200; I was just playing my shots.'

Rohit gave all the credit to his promotion as an opener and also the responsibility of leading Mumbai Indians.

'When you open you get a lot of opportunities to play more overs. I'm really relishing my new role. It's exciting and challenging. In the middle order, you don't get to play so many overs. The MI captaincy has brought about a big change in my batting. When you're given responsibility you change as an individual because people start expecting things out of you.'

The year 2013 ended on a bright note with that double century. Rohit had come a long way from the maidans of Mumbai to make some strong statements at some of the iconic venues of the world. 'I think he grew massively as a batsman in 2013. India was saying farewell to Sachin but here was a batsman who promised to take over the mantle,' said Kapil Dev, who loved the aggression that marked Rohit's batting. There was a resemblance in their approach to batting. Both believed they could excel on pitches that challenged the batsman with every ball and Rohit has carried this quality with consistency, shaping up exceedingly well against some of the most respected bowlers in international cricket.

Even though it continued to hurt Rohit that he was himself to blame for losing his place in the 2011 World Cup team, the focus was now to make the most of every contest. Of his 224 ODIs, Rohit played 137 matches with distinction until the game was brought to a halt due to the COVID-19 pandemic. That he scored 27 centuries in this fruitful phase is proof of his consistency. His average was 59.32. Rohit had finally established his credentials as one of the premier batsmen in limited overs cricket.

FIVE

The Making of The Hitman

The post-Tendulkar era had begun. Indian cricket had learnt to live without its most iconic cricketer. It was more than a year since Tendulkar last played in an ODI, the Asia Cup in Dhaka, and it was time for the selectors to have complete faith in Rohit stepping into the master's shoes.

Known critics of the game generally felt that Tendulkar should have called it a day in an ODI the day after India won the 2011 World Cup. That he continued was only a reflection of his intensity and wish to keep playing. For the first time in his illustrious career, he played far below his reputation. He was no longer the Tendulkar the world had known. Over seven Commonwealth Bank Series matches in Australia, he aggregated a disappointing 143 runs, with a highest score of 39.

When the Indian team for the Asia Cup was picked, Tendulkar did find a place on it even as criticism mounted at his insistence on extending his ODI career. On this occasion, however, he justified his presence and silenced his critics by contributing at crucial stages of India's campaign.

Tendulkar began with a score of six against Sri Lanka in the opening match, in which Gambhir and Kohli slammed a century each. His score of 114 failed to prevent a Bangladesh victory. The next outing, against Pakistan, saw Tendulkar reach a bristling 52, laying the base for an Indian win in a 133-run stand with Kohli. The win was small consolation, since it did not help India make it to the final where Pakistan beat Bangladesh to win the title. Tendulkar and Rohit, in a symbolic image of the new order in Indian cricket, crossed each other, with the latter contributing 68 as India won by four wickets. Tendulkar, who began his ODI career against Pakistan in 1989, ended it with an outing against the same opponent.

At the end of the Asia Cup, speculation surrounded Tendulkar's career. He was 12 short of the magical 200-Test mark, and India had a series lined up against New Zealand, England and Australia. The selectors continued to pick Tendulkar, and the Board backed him by staging a two-Test series against the West Indies, until he scaled the summit to become the first cricketer to play 200 Tests. Tendulkar's farewell series also witnessed the arrival of Rohit as a Test batsman. A century and a 'Man of the Match' award on debut, followed by another hundred, was a belated celebration of Rohit as a batsman to enjoy in the longest format of the game.

The ODI double century at Bengaluru had boosted Rohit's career. He could now afford to play with more freedom. The responsibilities increased manifold because he developed the reputation of a match-winner. He had the capacity to swing a match on his individual strength, and the Test debut was in keeping with his progress as a stroke player.

In becoming the 14th batsman to score a century on Test debut, Rohit emulated stalwarts like G.R. Viswanath, Mohammad Azharuddin, Sourav Ganguly and Virender Sehwag, to name a few. Azharuddin had lit up the Eden Gardens with a sterling century against England in 1984–1985, and Rohit won the hearts of the purists with a classical performance at one of the greatest theatres of world cricket.

Rohit took a mature approach, presented with the cap by Tendulkar. He avoided the compulsive desire to hit every ball. He was happy to play the waiting game and could pace his innings superbly once he applied his mind to the policy of playing the ball on merit. This was a new Rohit, and India was to benefit hugely from him.

'I am very happy to score on debut. A Test hundred is special,' said Rohit after the innings. He walked in at the fall of Tendulkar's wicket, 82 for four. A run later he lost Kohli too. Baptism by fire it was, and Rohit took charge without losing a moment. Rohit said, 'The wicket was really slow. Once the ball got older, it was not coming on. You got to hold back strokes and play late. Playing on the rise was not an ideal option on this wicket. There was a time three years ago when nothing was going right. Being a sportsman, there is a lot of inspiration to take from so many sportspersons from around the world. I knew once I get an opportunity, I would try and make the most of it. I just waited… kept working on my game. Today I am really happy with what has happened.'

Old-timers saw a bit of Azharuddin in Rohit. The desire to dominate, play shots off the legs, use delightful footwork against the spinners demonstrated the versatility of his batsmanship. He had made a dream start and attracted the attention of old-timers who valued good footwork. 'A batsman to watch out for,' was how Azharuddin welcomed Rohit's performance.

Challenges lay in store for Rohit when he played his next 12 Tests overseas—South Africa, New Zealand, England, Australia, Bangladesh and Sri Lanka. Former opener and coach Anshuman Gaekwad observed, 'The playing conditions in all these countries vary. The pitches test your technique and scoring skills. It was a tough test for Rohit because it is not easy to adapt. The bounce and swing can create problems for the best of batsmen and he had only just begun his Test career.'

Rohit ran into a bad patch. In 23 innings, he could aggregate just 582 run with four half-centuries, two of them coming against Sri Lanka. Statistics don't always speak the truth, but in Rohit's case they created immense pressure. The back-to-back centuries in his first two Tests set certain standards for the Mumbai batsman. Importantly, he could never get to open in any of those 12 Tests, and that did have an impact on his confidence.

'An opener's position is meant to be special. There are batsmen who have the mindset to stand up to the fastest of bowlers. You have to have the temperament to open and I felt for him because he had done well as an opener and then was denied the position,' said former opener Chetan Chauhan, reacting to Rohit's struggle in his overseas matches. Chauhan was fond of Rohit's batting for a simple reason: 'He loves to play shots and that gives him an advantage. Fast bowlers don't like being hit in the early stage of their spells.'

Not until Sri Lanka toured India in late 2017 did Rohit regain his confidence and composure. The opener slot remained elusive, and he found himself shackled in the middle order.

A brilliant knock of 102 not out against Sri Lanka at Nagpur in November 2017 was the only noteworthy Test innings to cement his place after a string of failures dented his confidence. The knock was part of a run-feast where Virat Kohli got a double century along with centuries by Cheteshwar Pujara and M. Vijay. Close to losing his place in the team, Rohit revived his Test career to survive the subsequent series against South Africa and Australia.

Rohit's place in the one-day team was secure since he was able to bat at his favourite position. Incidentally, his next century in ODIs after the Bengaluru feat was again a double century—264 against Sri Lanka at the Eden Gardens after a gap of 16 matches. A world-record performance, it was rated an all-time great ODI innings in the game. Rohit deserved the accolades that came his way as he broke Virender Sehwag's 2011 score of 219 against the West Indies at Indore. Tendulkar was the first batsman to reach that magical figure when he hit an unbeaten 200 against South Africa at Gwalior in 2010.

The knock by Rohit was paced like a true professional. He began slowly , reaching his 100 in the 32nd over, even playing out a maiden over. He had come to the match after recovering from a finger injury, but he was destined to make it big that day. He was lucky to have been dropped when at 4 off 18 balls. Once he realised fate was on his side, Rohit just exploded and his sixes came over cover as he timed the ball gloriously. In fact, he was hitting the ball at will in the latter half of his knock. His race to 250 was well documented by the statisticians—50 off 72 balls, the next 50 off 28. He took another 25 to reach 150 and 26 balls to herald the double century. And then Rohit just went berserk and treated the audience to some astonishing stroke play—50 coming off 15 balls. The Sri Lankans were left red-faced as India closed at 404 for five. Rohit sent off the last ball of the innings for a sensational knock that lasted 173 balls and included 33 fours and 9 sixes.

Rohit was on top of the world when he met the media after the innings. He said, 'I had to build the innings. The first 10 to 15 overs were not easy. I was feeling a little out of place. My strokes were not coming naturally. I wanted to stay in the middle and that required a lot of dedication and determination. I decided to stick around. Luckily, the quick-fire innings from Ajinkya Rahane helped me settle down. I just wanted to make my stay count. I wanted to make this game a special one for me and Team India.'

He also confessed to being mighty surprised when the team gave him an ovation. He added, 'I realised I must have passed the previous record (of 219) by (Virender) Sehwag. Most importantly I am happy to bat for 50 overs. To bat till last over is really pleasing for me. I have still a lot more to do. When I was young I wanted to play cricket. I never thought this would happen. But all the records happen along the way. I still have a lot more to do; probably work hard. The expectation could be more from here. A lot of responsibility on my shoulders.'

Rohit continued to grow as a massive hitter of the ball and smashed 10 more centuries before celebrating his third double in ODIs, again targeting the hapless Sri Lankan bowlers to script a 208 at Mohali in 2017. Among his big hundreds preceding that Mohali innings were 150 against South Africa in 2015, 171 not out against Australia at Perth in 2016 and 147 against New Zealand at Kanpur in 2017.

He was in peerless form at Perth, relishing the ball coming on the bat. Former India skipper Sourav Ganguly rated Rohit an amazing player. He said, 'He (Rohit) was exceptional, the way he batted. In one-day cricket and at top of the order he is as good as anybody in the world. He makes the game look easy when he gets going. He is an amazing player in the shorter format of the game. He is a terrific one-day player, and it surprises me that he does not turn this into big performances in Tests.'

Dhoni too paid rich compliments to Rohit. 'Whenever a batsman plays a long innings, the most important thing there is how he carries on once he gets to 50, then how he carries on once he gets to 100. Most times, when Rohit crosses 100–110 he scores quite big and that's always good. He is one of the players in the team who can play all the shots, exploit the field well, and hit effortlessly. It was a pity Rohit's knock went in vain as Australia hit back through Steve Smith (149) and George Bailey (112).'

Rohit's third double century came on the heels of a disastrous show by India at Dharamsala where Sri Lanka won by seven wickets after getting India out for 112. At one stage, India was 29 for seven and only Dhoni's 65 saved acute embarrassment.

The pitch at Mohali was tailor-made for Rohit as Sri Lanka made the mistake of putting India in to bat. What followed was a masterclass from Rohit, arguably the best one-day batsman of the times. His 208 off 153 balls was a package of highlights—13 fours and 12 sixes. The Sri Lankans just bowled and prayed, so merciless was the Indian opener.

Hailing the innings, former cricketer Vinod Kambli said on Twitter, 'Slaughter, slaughter, slaughter. Three double hundreds, an Amazing achievement. I am sure in the near future he

will be the first one to get 300,' even as Sehwag wrote, 'Wah Rohit Wah! 35 balls for the second hundred. So proud of you Rohit Sharma!'

Rohit agreed 2017 was his best year in international cricket as he reflected on his six ODI centuries. 'This year has been the best for me as a cricketer. I am only thinking about this particular series. I have been hitting the ball quite well. I had to be ready when the opportunity came. I have no regrets about what has happened in the past,' said Rohit.

The media was keen that Rohit rank his three double centuries, an exercise he was not keen on. 'The other two were as important as this one. The first one against Australia made it 2–2. For the one against Sri Lanka, I had returned from an injury. So for that reason it is right up there. Here we wanted to come back as a batting group. Also, it was my first stint as captain.'

There were suggestions that Rohit followed a pattern of scoring, pacing the innings after his first 100.

'The second hundred did not take that long because I was set. You understood what the bowlers were trying to do by then. It was all about playing according to the field. Once you get past 100, it is all about not making a mistake. There is no formula to it. The pitch was nice and hard and you could hit on the up. All the double hundreds I got were similar in pattern. I started off very slow and then picked up the pace, at the end I accelerated.'

Among the audience was his wife Ritika. Rohit rated the occasion as being very special. 'You must have seen on the screen that she was happier than me. She got a little emotional as well. It was the first double hundred she witnessed. It is

good to have her here. But more than that, winning the game is important.'

The year established Rohit as a premier ODI batsman of the world. He had come a long way from the debut match against Ireland in 2007 in which he did not even get to bat.

SIX

In a Zone of His Own

R ohit's rise in T20 cricket and the IPL is not surprising. His attacking style of batting and the confidence with which he destroys the best of bowlers made him a natural choice and a much sought-after player by the IPL franchises at the first IPL auction in February 2008. Five months earlier, he was a part of the victorious Indian team that won the inaugural ICC World T20 title in South Africa, finishing without an average as he aggregated 88 in three innings and remained not out in all three of them. He also had a healthy strike rate of 144.26. He scored 50 not out against South Africa at No. 5, 8 not out against Australia in the semi-final and 30 not out against Pakistan in the final, the last two coming at No. 6 behind skipper Mahendra Singh Dhoni.

Since he was an out-and-out Mumbaikar, it may have come as a surprise that Rohit was picked up by the Hyderabad-based Deccan Chargers owned by Deccan Chronicle Holdings Ltd. in the first auction for USD 7,50,000 (then approx. Rs 3 crore), half the price of what Chennai Super Kings bought their future youth icon player Dhoni for.

What increased Rohit's worth in the IPL auction was his performance in the CB series in Australia a few days earlier. He played a couple of match-winning knocks including the 66 in the company of the legendary Sachin Tendulkar in the first of three finals against Australia in Sydney.

Rohit joined Tendulkar at 87/3 with India chasing 240 to win. After sharing 123 with the Master Blaster Tendulkar, where Sachin reached his masterly century, and taking India to the doorstep of victory, Rohit fell. With this knock, he proved he was indispensable in international cricket. It was a pleasing sight to see the veteran and the rookie go about punishing the Australian bowlers, the guru guiding his *shishya* in the business of taking on the opposition.

India won that first final by six wickets and went on to win the second in Brisbane two days later by nine runs, with Tendulkar making 91. This was India's first ever tri-series title triumph in Australia, and Rohit had a crucial hand in it.

While accepting his 'Man of the Match' award for his unbeaten 117 in the first final, Tendulkar spoke highly of Rohit: 'Rohit Sharma really batted well. Full credit to him. He has a terrific head on his shoulders. He's calm and composed, and today I batted with him for the first time for such a long time (108 minutes of entertaining partnership).'[1]

This knock went a long way in boosting Rohit's career. Like Rohit's contemporary, Bengal batsman and captain Manoj Tiwary, said, 'As far as Rohit and his opportunities are concerned, whatever I have seen by touring with him and sharing the dressing room with him, he basically grabs them with both hands. Like the way the opportunities came his way in Australia. That has paved the way for his international career.'[2]

Tiwary, who captained Rohit in the India Under-19 series against England in the home series in 2004–2005, made his ODI debut in the same CB series in Australia that brought Rohit to the fore.

Tiwary said, 'Rohit played outstandingly well in the CB series, where I missed out on the first game in Brisbane (although I had reached the venue the previous day). Missing out on the opportunity (Manoj played this game in Brisbane within hours of landing in Australia and was bowled by a brutal Brett Lee yorker for two) in the first game did not give the captain and management enough confidence in me.

'On the other side, Rohit played a couple of good knocks in that series. That has taken his career going in international cricket. Not only did he play well, but he also made good contributions with Sachin *paaji*. Any cricketer, whether experienced or newcomer, batting with Sachin *paaji* and making a good partnership, and that game ends up in India's way, that knock and the player get more highlighted. This is because the "God of Cricket" is playing at the other end. When Sachin *paaji* appreciates anyone's knock, it has more weightage. That's how it started in his case. Rohit would be greatly nurtured by none other than Tendulkar when he played alongside one of the greatest icons of the game, in both the Indian team and later in the IPL with Mumbai Indians from 2011. Tendulkar's continued association with Mumbai Indians has helped Rohit grow as a captain as well.'

Thus rose Rohit's worth in the IPL. He became indispensable as an IPL player and grew into the most successful captain in the history of the cash-rich cricket league. His stock also rose,

making him one of the most expensive IPL players—he was retained by Mumbai Indians for Rs 15 crore in the 2018 auction.

It may seem strange to associate Rohit with Deccan Chargers. But relatives from his mother's side saw it a homecoming of sorts as his mother Purnima hails from the port city of Visakhapatnam.

Rohit did not disappoint his new fan base in the south with his batting performance. He had a fairly decent average of 36.72 in the first season of the IPL for Deccan Chargers, second in the list of most runs scored for his team (404) behind the captain, the marauding Australian wicketkeeper-batsman Adam Gilchrist (436).

Rohit is the only person to have tasted five IPL titles out of a maximum of 12—one with Deccan Chargers as a player in 2009 in South Africa and four as captain of Mumbai Indians.

Each title was hard earned. After having a forgettable maiden season with Deccan Chargers, the Gilchrist-led team did a dramatic turnaround when the IPL went to South Africa in 2009, its second year, as it coincided with the General Elections in India and not enough security could be provided.

In a season in which Rohit played crucial knocks to accumulate 362 runs in Deccan Chargers' triumphant run, he also played a handy role with the ball, bowling off-spinners. His most significant performance with the ball came in Centurion against his future IPL team, Mumbai Indians, when he took a hat-trick, much to his own surprise.

The hat-trick came in the last two balls of the 16th over and the first ball of the 18th, Rohit's first and second over in that match. He clean bowled his close friend Abhishek Nayar, followed by Harbhajan Singh. He then had South African J.P. Duminy caught behind to complete a hat-trick. He did not

realise this until his team-mate, Australian Ryan Harris, brought it to his notice.

During the COVID-19 lockdown in 2020, Rohit admitted that he was even embarrassed about taking that hat-trick. Rohit told Australian David Warner in a chat on Instagram Live, 'I can't believe that, man, I seriously can't believe that I took a hat-trick against Mumbai Indians while I was playing for Deccan Chargers. I don't even remember how I used to bowl then. I got a finger injury and after that I could not grip the ball properly. And these days, it's better to stay away from bowling. If I think of it now, it's quite embarrassing that I took a hat-trick. They were decent batters as well.'[3]

That hat-trick was actually Rohit's second. 'I took a hat-trick for my school, Swami Vivekananda, in the Harris Shield as a 14-year-old. I remember that match very well as I had also scored 123 and taken six wickets, the hat-trick included,' said Rohit in the post-match media briefing, with the first of 17 IPL 'Man of the Match' awards by his side.[4]

Rohit finished with impressive figures of 4/6 in 2 overs to add to his 38 in Deccan Chargers' total of 145/6.

Deccan Chargers captain Gilchrist did not consider Rohit to be a part-time bowler in that successful campaign. 'I don't think there are part-time bowlers in T20. Rohit bowled in just about every game. You have got to be versatile in T20. His bowling late in pressure situations helped,' the Aussie said.

By his own admission, Rohit said then that he did not like being called a part-timer: 'I have been bowling for long now. I have the confidence. I have bowled quite a bit for Mumbai and India.'

Rohit collected his second IPL 'Man of the Match' award 10 days later against Kolkata Knight Riders at the Wanderers. Walking in at 116/3 in the 17th over with the Chargers needing another 45 runs from 22 balls, Rohit played a blinder. His 13-ball unbeaten 32, with three fours and two sixes, sealed a last-ball finish for the eventual champions.

The Chargers needed 21 off the last over sent down by Bangladesh's Mashrafe Mortaza. A four off a no-ball to start the over eased the pressure off Rohit. A leg-bye single and a run off his partner Y. Venugopala Rao's blade from the next two legal deliveries brought down the equation to 14 needed off four deliveries. And, with Rohit on strike, it was easily achievable. That's what Rohit believed.

And he did it in style, with a six off the third delivery over mid-wicket off a juicy full toss followed by a wide off the next. This put the pressure back on Mortaza and KKR. A couple balls down the ground made it to five off the last two. A wide and full from Mortaza was dispatched for four to level the scores.

Not satisfied by just taking a single and knock off the winning run, Rohit rubbed salt into KKR's wounds by pulling a short ball behind square to seal the win with a six.

'There was pressure, but the wicket was good to bat on. When I hit a boundary off the first ball (of the last over), a no-ball, I then thought the target was quite gettable. I feel very happy to contribute to the team's win,' Rohit said after collecting his 'Man of the Match' award.

Not only had his efforts with the bat and ball grown in stature by then, but his reading of the game and the situation

had grown greatly. Having successfully defended 145 to win by 19 runs in the game in which he took a hat-trick, Rohit said that chasing under lights a total in the 140–150 range would be difficult.

'I have been following this tournament very closely, and it is not easy to chase under lights. You have to first settle down and then go after the attack in the last five overs. Anything between 140 and 150 is a good total,' Sharma said.

How true that statement held two-and-a-half weeks later! Chargers defended a total of 143/6 against Royal Challengers under lights at the Wanderers to lift their only IPL title. What a turnaround after finishing last in the table in the previous season! Rohit had a huge role to play in it.

In his last year with Deccan Chargers in 2010, Rohit scored 404 but could not take them beyond the semi-finals, losing to eventual champions Chennai Super Kings in the last four and also bowing down to RCB in the third-place play-off.

Thus ended Rohit's association with the Hyderabad franchise. In the 45 matches for Deccan Chargers, Rohit scored close to 1,200 runs, averaging nearly 31 with eight 50s. The fact that he could not score a single century for the Chargers in the IPL was because he batted in the middle or lower-middle order with only a few overs remaining.

In the 2011 auction, the first since 2008, he was bought by Mumbai Indians for USD 2 million (approx. Rs 9.2 crore) after a bidding war with Deccan Chargers and Kings XI Punjab. His love-affair with the Reliance-owned team only strengthened with every year, and the two became inseparable, what with MI retaining him for Rs 15 crore before the 2018 auction.

Rohit and Mumbai Indians

Mumbai Indians looked at Rohit as one for the future, and maybe they also looked at him as a captain material at that point of time. Rohit felt like a complete Mumbaikar when MI picked him up for USD 1.25 million more than what DC were giving him.

Soon after the January 2011 auction, Rohit said that it felt great to be back in Mumbai. 'I was expecting to be picked for a decent amount. If you look at the overall statistics, you'll know that I am the third highest run-getter in the IPL. Maybe that record worked in my favour,' he said.

Rohit was aware that he would not be retained by DC before the auctions. And what a blessing it turned out to be for Rohit! He said, 'They (DC officials) told me they won't retain me but will surely go for me at the auction. Mumbai Indians told me the same thing. Actually, I am happy to play for Mumbai Indians. I have played for Mumbai (the domestic side) for five years now. Now I am a complete Mumbaikar.'

Regarding the privilege of sharing the dressing room with Tendulkar in the IPL as well, Rohit said, 'I share a very, very close relationship with him and this will only help me learn more from him. It's a feeling I can't explain. And this is something I was waiting for,' he said.[5]

Rohit had faced the disappointment of not being picked for the 2011 World Cup, even though this was largely his own doing, as he did not have enough runs in the ODI series leading up to the mega event. Being picked up by Mumbai Indians in the IPL 2011 auction acted as a soothing ointment.

Following his back-to-back ODI hundreds in Zimbabwe soon after the 2010 IPL, Rohit's form slumped to the extent that in the next 16 ODI innings, he managed only one 50, two 40s and a 30+. In these 16 innings, his average was a poor 18.125.

Chatting with England's Kevin Pietersen on Instagram during the 2020 lockdown, Rohit answered a question regarding the lowest point of his career: 'Not getting picked for the 2011 World Cup squad, that was the saddest moment as it was happening in our own backyard, the final was played at my home ground. It was due to my performances, I was not at my best.'[6]

Rohit continued making fine contributions in his first IPL season for Mumbai Indians, coming largely at No. 4 and lending the balance between the top-order and the lower order and trying to bat till the end overs, something that he would do regularly until the 2018 IPL.

Rohit's first fifty-plus score for MI—48-ball 87 (8x4, 5x6)—lit up his home ground Wankhede Stadium and set up for an exciting match, defeating the defending champions Chennai Super Kings by eight runs. His performance was outmatched with the ball by Harbhajan Singh, who picked up 5/18 in 4 overs to stop CSK's march despite S. Badrinath's fighting unbeaten 71.

He followed his first MI 50 with a 56 against his old team Deccan Chargers two days later on Tendulkar's birthday in Hyderabad. Yet again, his batting exploits were pipped by Lasith Malinga's bowling efforts (3/9) in the comfortable 37-run MI victory.

It was against his old team DC that Rohit won his first 'Man of the Match' award for MI. This was in the 2012 season. His 50-ball 73 not out (4×4, 5×6) came in a dramatic fashion, resulting

in a last-ball finish. Chasing the Chargers' 138/9, MI needed 18 off the final over, and New Zealand's James Franklin, no muck with the bat, faced the first ball. Rohit needed to be on strike, which he did only from the fourth delivery when the Kiwi stole a bye off the third ball against Daniel Christian's medium pace. When Rohit took a strike from the fourth ball, MI needed another 11 runs to win. The first ball he faced was a full toss swung mightily over point for six. After a two in the next ball, the equation was down to three off the last ball. Rohit gobbled up another Christian full toss, depositing it over long on for a six.

His first 'Man of the Match' performance for MI could not have come against a better team and in a better situation!

However, the first IPL century from as talented a batsman as Rohit was elusive. Yes, he was batting at No. 4, and the opportunity to score a century did not arise. However, the first, and only, IPL century in Rohit's 188-match IPL career—109 not out against Kolkata Knight Riders at his favourite venue Eden Gardens—came towards the end of the fifth edition of the IPL.

It was his 74th IPL match, and 29th with Mumbai Indians. He walked in to bat in the third over after Tendulkar fell for 2. Thereafter, it was chasing leather for KKR for the rest of the 17.4 overs as Rohit and his old mate from Deccan Chargers, Herschelle Gibbs, shared an undefeated 167 with the South African's contribution being 66 not out in 58 balls, two balls less than what Rohit faced.

The two MI batsmen took the game away from KKR, and they won by a handsome 27 runs.

The proud Man of the Match Rohit said at the presentation that there was no game plan and that he wanted to bat a full 20 overs. This belief and strategy would go on to feature regularly over the coming years for both MI and India that he had become a dangerous limited overs batsman the world over.

'Wanted to go there and spend some time, which is what usually helps. Wanted to bat 20 overs. We were batting first and wanted to get a decent target. Managed to keep wickets in hands, which helped,' Rohit said.[7]

His opposition captain Gautam Gambhir could only applaud Rohit's knock and pity his bowlers for the onslaught. 'It was an outstanding innings from Rohit. The bowling had been doing well and this was one of those off days. If someone plays such kind of knocks, you cannot do a lot.'

Rohit has always put his team's interests ahead of his personal goals. He sacrificed his favourite opening slot to bat in the middle, at No. 4, to lend balance and strength in the end overs. He had to make this adjustment for the IPL even as he was opening for India in the ODIs with Shikhar Dhawan from the 2013 Champions Trophy and almost regularly from the start in T20Is.

'IPL is different from international cricket. I spoke before the start of IPL that to give balance to the team, I will bat lower down,' Rohit said a day after leading MI to their third IPL title in May 2017.

While he batted at No. 4 for MI, he had to adapt quickly to opening the batting in the ensuing Champions Trophy in England in 2017. 'I don't think it is going to be difficult to adapt at this age. All it needs is to develop the mindset,' Rohit said.

Rohit's IPL career was to take a significant turn in the 2013 IPL. He took over the captaincy from the under-performing Ricky Ponting and led the side to its first title. Rohit himself came up with loads of runs befitting his growing stature, scoring in excess of 500 runs and playing some crucial knocks at No. 4.

Rohit's importance in the MI set up began to grow immensely as the franchise built its team with its trusted lieutenants. Lasith Malinga, Kieron Pollard, Ambati Rayudu were becoming MI's pillars. With Rohit as captain, the team would develop into a formidable unit.

The year 2013 also saw Tendulkar play his last IPL match and step out of the league as a player with an IPL title that eluded him in the first five seasons. It was later in 2013 that Tendulkar would retire from the international scene; his farewell Tests against the West Indies in November that year would mark the introduction of Rohit into Tests. Rohit made a remarkable entry into the longest format, scoring back-to-back centuries in his first two Tests, 177 at Eden Gardens and 111 not out at the Wankhede.

Defending their title in the IPL 2014, MI were off to an inauspicious start, losing all their first five games in the UAE, where the first part of the IPL was played due to General Elections in India. It was moved back to the country later. On the slow pitches of Dubai, Abu Dhabi and Sharjah, Mumbai lost to Kolkata Knight Riders by 41 runs, Royal Challengers Bangalore by seven wickets, CSK by seven wickets, Delhi Daredevils (rechristened to Delhi Capitals in early 2019) by six wickets and CSK again by 15 runs.

Their batting failed to click even as the bowlers delivered the goods. Even changing the batting order with Rohit as opener in the last game outside India did not work.

Rohit did not come up with good scores either, except for a 41-ball 50 against CSK. Three single-digit scores from his blade in the UAE did not help MI's cause either. Played five, lost five for MI before the India leg commenced.

Once the IPL returned to India, their fortunes turned around for the better. MI won seven of their next nine league matches to finish fourth in the table and qualify for the play-offs, where they were knocked out in the eliminator by CSK.

'We showed a lot of character after losing the first five games. Coming back to India and performing like that was incredible,' Rohit said after the eliminator loss. He too pulled up his socks to notch up a couple of fifties, one score in the forties and a couple of thirties.

In the brief existence of the Champions League T20 from 2009 to 2014, Rohit led Mumbai Indians to its second title, in 2013, to complete a double along with the IPL title. In 2011, MI had the third edition of the T20 League that had the champion T20 teams from Australia, South Africa, England and the West Indies.

Rohit played two CLT20 matches for Deccan Chargers in 2009, but it was in 2013 that he played a couple of significant knocks, including an unbeaten 51 against Perth Scorchers, to take MI into the semi-finals. Chasing Scorchers' 149/6, MI cruised home in just the 14th over with Rohit smashing his half-century in just 23 balls with three fours and four sixes at No. 4, picking up the 'Man of the Match' award as well.

A shoulder injury, adding to the middle-finger injury sustained in England during India's tour, forced Rohit out of the 2014 CLT20. After this edition, which was won by Chennai Super Kings for the second time, CLT20 was scrapped due to lack of interest among the public.[8]

There were no such issues with the IPL, and Rohit continued to bat for MI in IPL at No. 4 with the team's larger interest in mind. This continued until the end of 2018 IPL, winning the 2015 and 2017 titles in the process as well.

Rohit had a fabulous IPL 2015 as a captain, beginning with an unbeaten 98 as an opener against KKR at his beloved venue, Eden Gardens, though the knock ended on the losing side with the home team chasing down 168/3 with nine balls to spare. This was the first of four straight defeats for MI, which was once again having problems starting out in the league.

Following their opening seven-wicket loss to KKR, MI went down to Kings XI Punjab by 18 runs, Rajasthan Royals by seven wickets and Chennai Super Kings by six wickets. Their first win, by just 18 runs, came against Royal Challengers Bangalore.

However, Rohit ended up with a man-of-the-match performance in the final against CSK, also in Kolkata, powering MI to their second IPL title.

Rohit opened for MI in 2015 in the first game before going back to his No. 4 slot in some of the games and to No. 3 towards the end of the tournament as well as in the final. By now, as the scorer of two ODI double hundreds—including the highest ever by an individual in this format, 264 against Sri Lanka at Eden Gardens—Rohit's stock had grown manifold, and expectations from him were immense.

Rohit's move to shift to the middle order worked in MI's successful campaign as the West Indian Lendl Simmons took the responsibility of making the most of the powerplay at the top of the batting order and getting the team off to a flier.

Rohit's 50 in 26 balls in the final made the difference in MI posting a defendable total. Useful contributions from Kieron Pollard and Ambati Rayudu ensured MI crossed 200, which proved too much even for the 'finisher' Dhoni and CSK, such that MI eventually won by 41 runs.

Mumbai Indians failed to defend their IPL title yet again in 2016, the year in which the league was moved out of their home ground Wankhede after the first four matches due to an acute drought situation. Visakhapatnam became MI's home ground. MI failed to qualify for the play-offs, winning seven and losing seven to finish fifth in the table.

As MI played all their home games at their fortress in Mumbai in 2017, their confidence also returned. They went on to win five of their seven home matches, qualified for the play-offs by finishing first in the table, thereby getting two chances for a place in the final. They lost the Qualifier 1 to Rising Pune Supergiant by 20 runs but defeated KKR in Qualifier 2 to enter the title round, where they defeated RPS by one run.

In 2019, for the first time since the IPL began, the 50-over ICC Cricket World Cup was being held after the IPL. The 2011 and 2015 World Cups were held before the IPL and so there had not been much to worry about.

IPL 2019 was looked at as a preparation for the World Cup in England in June–July, and Rohit had decided to open for MI.

When asked at the 2019 MI pre-season press conference if he would open for MI even as he would be opening in the World Cup, the skipper said, 'This year, I will open the batting for all the games. That is for sure. World Cup is one of the factors. Also keeping in mind that this is where I bat when I play for India. And, that is where I have got a lot of success of late.'[9]

Not only did he prepare well for the World Cup but also led MI with aplomb for their fourth IPL title, with a one-run win over Chennai Super Kings in Hyderabad being the icing on the cake. Rohit then went on to make the ICC World Cup his own, scoring centuries at will, five of them in a single edition, one more than what Sri Lanka's Kumar Sangakkara had done in the 2015 edition in Australia and New Zealand.

SEVEN

Leading from the Front

Australian captain Ricky Ponting, who led his country to two back-to-back ICC 50-over Cricket World Cup titles in 2003 and 2007, was acquired in the 2013 player auction for USD 4,00,000 and named MI captain. He took over the mantle from Harbhajan Singh, who could not carry his team beyond the eliminator stage in 2012. Rohit was two IPL seasons old with Mumbai Indians at the time.

Chief mentor of MI and legendary leg-spinner Anil Kumble explained Ponting's appointment as captain thus: 'Ricky has a lot of experience to lead a competitive and a high-profile side like Mumbai Indians in the IPL. Sachin readily agreed to my suggestion that Mumbai Indians is best served when he leads the batting unburdened by the rigours of captaincy. It was our idea (Sachin and mine) to bring in Ricky as the captain of the Mumbai Indians.'

While welcoming Ponting into the leadership group, MI owner Nita Ambani said, 'We have world's two biggest cricketing greats in Sachin and Ricky, and I am sure the duo will be an inspiration for the youngsters in the team.

'Sachin will always be an integral and important part of Mumbai Indians' leadership. Ricky will bring in fresh perspective in the team leadership and will have the support of the best cricketing minds like Sachin, Anil and John Wright.'

Accepting the captaincy, the Tasmanian said, 'It's a huge honour and I thank Mrs Ambani and the Mumbai Indians management for the faith they have reposed in my abilities. Mumbai Indians has the potent combination of Indian and international cricketers and I look forward to leading the team to play to its full potential.'[10]

Ponting was not cut out to play T20s. Or so it seemed. It was like expecting a polished diamond like Rahul Dravid to play Virender Sehwag-style in T20 cricket. And, at 38, already out of international cricket, Ponting's experience and knowledge was what was sought after by MI management.

Ponting's only IPL experience before MI picked him up in 2013 was in the inaugural edition for Kolkata Knight Riders, when he averaged only 9.75 in the four matches he played.

Ponting and Tendulkar opened for Mumbai Indians. You would expect fireworks from two of the greatest batsmen of the modern era, especially when they opened the batting. But the pressure to quickly score runs was getting to them.

Barring the 52-run stand that the two raised in the first match against RCB in Bengaluru in 7.3 overs, there was little of note from the two in terms of partnership. Ponting could not inspire the team to victory in his first game as MI skipper as RCB won by two runs.

After further failures, even though Mumbai had three wins under Ponting, largely thanks to Rohit's contributions with the

bat in two of them—it was time for the Aussie to drop out on his own.

Who else could MI think of from the available lot other than Rohit as captain from the seventh match onwards? As Rohit revealed in mid-May 2020 in an Instagram Live chat with his Test team-mate and off-spinner Ravichandran Ashwin, wicketkeeper-batsman Dinesh Karthik had been another candidate for captaincy! Rohit told Ashwin, 'I was part of the Pragyan Ojha trade from Deccan Chargers and that's when I thought I could be captain. I thought I have to be ready when the opportunity comes my way. They got Ponting in the auction (in 2013). I can't compete with him. Some people were thinking we can go with DK. But Ponting called me and said I want you to take it forward.'

Rohit could not stop praising Ponting. He said, 'I feel Ponting is a guy from another planet. He knows how to bring out the best in someone. He has won two World Cups for Australia (as captain, 2003 and 2007). So he knows how to win Championships.

'In 2013, we got Ricky Ponting in the auction. In 2012 Sachin *paaji* said that he would not lead Mumbai Indians and Bhajju paa (Harbhajan) was made the skipper. But in 2013, I don't know why Bhajju paa wasn't the captain. And I thought I will be made the captain, but then Ponting was bought in the auction.

'Ponting was the first one to arrive in India for the 2013 season. He wanted to understand everyone. He said that he wanted to have a team bonding session first. In a way, it made a very positive impact on everyone. Ponting really motivated the younger guys. But then he was not scoring runs, he decided to

step down as the skipper, but eventually Ponting called me and I was given the captaincy. Ponting actually was player-cum-coach during the 2013 season. He was always there to help me.'[11]

Rohit was also in fine form with the bat. Under Ponting, he had scored a masterly unbeaten 74 and raised 132 with Dinesh Karthik for the third wicket against Delhi Daredevils after both the legendary openers fell with only one on the board.

Rohit followed this with a man-of-the-match performance of 62 not out in 32 balls with three fours and five sixes against Pune Warriors.

MI could not have got a better captain than in-form Rohit, aged 26 at the time and carrying a mature head on his shoulders. Rohit could not have found a more auspicious time than 24 April 2013, the day the person called the 'God of Cricket' turned 40, to take over the reins of a team full of high-profile players.

It was a rainy evening in Kolkata on 24 April 2013, the day MI were to take on KKR. The start was delayed by half an hour. Rohit walked out for the 8 pm toss, with play scheduled to start at 8.30 pm. Gautam Gambhir and Ricky Ponting had pulled out of the playing XI. It seemed that the rain gods had showered their blessings on Rohit, who was starting on a new journey in his IPL career as skipper.

It was becoming a trend in the IPL that non-performing players, first choice in their national sides, dropped themselves from the playing XI so as to give more promising ones a chance and not be a burden to the side. The IPL, after all, is about instant results. Kumar Sangakkara, Angelo Mathews, Sanath Jayasuriya and Glenn McGrath had either been dropped by their respective franchises for not performing or had not been given a game at all, as in the case of the Australian legendary paceman.

Ponting was facing the ire of not delivering the goods with the bat—he had scores of 28, 6, 0, 14 and 4 in the first five matches he played before not going out to bat in the sixth match against Delhi Daredevils at the Ferozeshah Kotla in New Delhi, now renamed as Arun Jaitley Stadium.

It was a sign of things to come, having legends of the game in Tendulkar, Ponting, Kumble, Wright among others in the dressing room and to grow as a captain. Rohit was blessed to be in that surrounding.

Mumbai Indians have had some great players as captain in the past, but none could inspire the team to perform better than Rohit did. Legends in their own right, Tendulkar, Harbhajan and Ponting led Mumbai Indians, and it was under them that Rohit developed and developed his captaincy skills. While Harbhajan may have been given the captaincy for his stature in Indian cricket, the other two have had contrasting results as captains of their respective national teams.

But leading in the IPL was a different ball game. Rohit allowed youngsters to play freely and gave them confidence, as with Nitish Rana in 2017 and Rahul Chahar in 2019. Of course, Bumrah and the Pandya brothers, among others, were a regular feature in the MI set up, blossoming under Rohit's captaincy.

Even in tense situations, when you would suspect the game was slipping from MI's grasp and Rohit's thinking was going astray, you could trust him to come up with something different as captain. It could be in the form of a bowling change or a field placement, or just giving the depleted bowler another over and showing his faith in them to deliver the goods. Or simply, an acrobatic catch in the outfield would give Rohit relief and bring the game back on track.

Rohit lost his first toss as IPL captain. MI were made to chase as KKR captain Gautam Gambhir chose to bat. Rohit himself, coming at No. 4, made 34 and gave the explosive West Indian Dwayne Smith solid support as MI successfully chased KKR's challenging 159/6.

However, it was not an auspicious start to his captaincy, as he lost the toss and Harbhajan, opening the bowling, was smashed for 4, 4, 4 and 6 by the marauding Yusuf Pathan off the first four balls of the match.

His bowlers Lasith Malinga, Mitchell Johnson and Pragyan Ojha brought the team back on track, thus restricting KKR to a total that was eventually achievable in the match's penultimate delivery, with half the side not required to bat.

Rohit was pleased and relieved to win his first match as MI captain. He said after the match, 'Good start to captaincy, happy with the way we fought. Didn't get a good start but the comeback was superb. We always knew that we have guys who could get us back into the game.'[12]

On accepting the captaincy, Rohit said post-match, 'I felt really good when the management handed over the responsibility to me. I was nervous as this was the first time I was leading Mumbai Indians. All that nervousness went away off when I entered the field because I wanted to concentrate on what I needed to do. It is a short format, you need to keep thinking. Am very happy the way I approached the game.'

Rohit said that it was Ponting's personal decision to step down from the playing XI and never to appear again in an IPL game. 'It was his personal decision. It takes a lot of heart and guts to do that. We felt we wanted to get the right combination

and he was the one who stood up and said, "I will not be playing this game,"' Rohit said.[13]

Ponting's involvement with MI for the rest of the 2015 season culminated in the team winning their second IPL title. Being captain helped greatly in the Mumbaikar's growth.

When MI retained Ponting for the next three seasons, 2014 to 2016, Rohit grew as a captain, which enabled him to lead MI to two more titles in 2017 and 2019 under their new coach, Sri Lanka's Mahela Jayawardena.

Rohit, in a recent Instagram Live session with Pietersen, singled out Ponting as the best coach he played under in IPL. Rohit said, 'Very difficult to pick one name because they all bring something or the other to the table. But Ricky Ponting, to me, was magic. The way he handled the team when he was captain for the first half, and then gave it to me, it takes a lot of guts to do that.

'After that as well, to be as involved as he was, as a member of the support staff. He was helping all the youngsters and guided me through the captaincy. I got to learn a lot from him. He was a different ball game altogether.'[14]

Ponting also received a thumbs up from owner Nita Ambani in mentoring the youngsters and grooming Rohit. In an interview to the now-defunct newspaper *DNA* in April 2015, Ambani said, 'We also have Ricky Ponting as the head coach this year. As a captain and player during 2013, Ricky has been a thorough professional in his approach to the game and the way he motivates others around him. For someone like Ricky, who led Australia to two World Cup victories, to step down from captaincy for the team's goal, is a selfless and commendable act.'[15]

The successful Australian captain, a legendary batsman, was pleased with the way Rohit has led the team in the IPL. He said in 2015, 'Rohit's captaincy has been spot on. In 2013 when we won the title, he took over the captaincy from me and the way he controlled the players on the field is fantastic. He understands the game really well and communicates with the players well.'[16]

While at the bottom of his heart Rohit wanted to open for MI, he came at the top of the order only if there was no other suitable player to do the job. Lending balance to the middle and lower-order was still his major worry, and he was best suited for that.

West Indies' Lendl Simmons, who played a crucial role in knocking India out of the 2016 ICC T20 World Cup in India, was ruled out of the rest of IPL 2016 after the first game. The aggressive New Zealander Martin Guptill was named Simmons' replacement, but he got to play only in three matches, obviously not being the first-choice opener.

Rohit moved up and down the order in the tournament depending on the composition of the playing XI, opening most times with the left-handed wicketkeeper-batsman Parthiv Patel while dropping himself back to No. 4 on the odd occasion.

Rohit's best knocks in 2016 came when he was the opener. He batted from first ball to anchor the successful run chase in pursuit of KKR's 187/5 at Eden Gardens, making 84 not out from just 54 balls with 10 fours and two sixes. Another man-of-the-match innings of 62 came against RCB at the Wankhede while chasing a target of 171 with two overs to spare. He followed these with two back-to-back man-of-the-match performances of 68 not out against KKR and 85 not out against RPS in successful

run chases, batting from ball one and staying till the end in both the matches.

In 2016, when the IPL was shifted out of Mumbai as Maharashtra was facing a drought, MI's chances of qualifying for playoffs also reduced. Mumbai Indians have had a greater success percentage in Mumbai, having won 30 of the 41 matches in all in 2008, 2010, 2011, 2012 and 2013. In fact, they won all their eight home matches in 2013 en route to their maiden IPL title.

At the start of the season, Rohit explained the decision to open in IPL 2016 thus: 'It's important to get the balance and the position of each player right, where they have batted for their country/state, it's important to keep that going.

'For me, I've been opening for a while—three years now—so I'd like to continue that for the remainder of the series. But everything depends on the balance, if I feel me batting top of order is not right for the team, I'll come down as a middle-order batsman. If it helps the team, I'm ready to do whatever it takes to help the team win. We have to share the responsibility. I cannot be just one person winning the tournament.'

Nevertheless, Rohit would drop down to No. 3 or 4 for the whole of 2017 and 2018, barring the first two matches, in which he opened with the West Indian Evin Lewis. With the team well set and MI having a lot of power hitters in the middle and lower order in Kieron Pollard, the Pandya brothers and Suryakumar Yadav, Rohit could afford to open for the entire 2019 season. Another factor was that he was going to open for the country in the World Cup that followed the IPL.

When Rohit opened with South African wicketkeeper-batsman Quinton de Kock, the duo often gave their team the

start it needed. This was crucial to MI winning their fourth IPL title, something that no team has done before, moving one ahead of Dhoni's CSK while KKR came third with two titles. For the record, Rajasthan Royals, Deccan Chargers (for whom Rohit played in 2008, 2009 and 2010) and Sunrisers Hyderabad complete the list of IPL winners.

Rohit was always the players' captain. He gave them a free hand, let the bowlers have their field and believed in their abilities. It was this trait that made youngsters and seniors alike love playing under him. Being a happy-go-lucky guy, he was not a dictator like some leaders. Rohit believed in his players' abilities. It was under him that players such as Hardik Pandya and Jasprit Bumrah blossomed and have now become major attractions in world cricket. Players from other countries too have benefitted from playing under Rohit's captaincy.

Young left-spinner Rahul Chahar, who played a crucial hand in MI's title win in 2019, played 14 matches in the team's successful run, picking up 13 wickets including two three-fors. He credited Rohit for his rise as a cricketer and thanked his IPL captain after earning his maiden national call-up in 2019 against the West Indies in the Caribbean islands.

The 20-year-old Chahar said last year, 'Rohit *bhaiya* showed trust in me. Be it powerplays or death overs, he never hesitated to give me the ball. He said "...*jaise hamesha daalta hai, waise daalna* (bowl the way you always do)." I have bowled in the second over of a match and also the 17th over. The two are very different situations. This shows that Rohit bhaiya was confident about my bowling. He also said, "*Mujhe pata hai tu run nahi jaane dega* (I know you won't concede too many runs)." He knew I can control the flow of runs. He is an amazing captain.'[17]

So what made Rohit a successful captain? His best friend from the Under-16 days and Mumbai Ranji Trophy team-mate Abhishek Nayar put it in a single word: 'preparation'.[18]

Nayar explained, 'Rohit's preparation towards captaincy and his ability to let the players be and feel secure in a team atmosphere is his biggest strength. Those two aspects for me stand out in his leadership.'

Despite being a a happy-go-lucky, fun-loving guy, Rohit took his cricket seriously. Along with his talent and knowledge, these features combined to make Rohit a players' captain. Nayar continued, 'Preparation, he always had in his cricket. That translated into captaincy. In terms of the security aspect, looking at his mannerisms as an individual, he has never been an insecure person. When you are not an insecure person, it rubs off on your teammates. He knows he is not worried about what someone is doing or not doing, he does what he needs to do, prepares hard enough to execute his plans. He keeps it very simple.'

Nayar played in three ODIs in 2009 but was more a gutsy player for Mumbai in their Ranji Trophy-winning campaigns. He subsequently played in 60 IPL matches for a total of four teams—Rajasthan Royals, Kings XI Punjab, Mumbai Indians and Pune Warriors—between 2008 and 2014.

Currently assistant coach of KKR, Nayar knows Rohit more closely than anyone else. 'Leading MI to four IPL titles is no joke. Rohit would do anything for the team without any second thought. He is a nice guy. No question about that,' he said.

Manoj Tiwary, a player who could have been a contemporary of Rohit but lost out on opportunities due to an injury and was then left out of the Indian team when he was growing in confidence from the limited chances he got, commented on

Rohit's captaincy thus: 'I was a little surprised by his captaincy skills. I did not notice, in our India U-19 days, his leadership skills. That said, the responsibility of captaincy has made him a better player.'

'It could not have been a better team to lead. When you have superstars in the team, when Sachin Tendulkar is associated with any team, any young captain like Rohit will benefit. Add to it the likes of other people associated with him in the MI dressing room—Ricky Ponting, Anil Kumble and other great players. He has gained a lot of confidence from these great players and taken their advice in a positive way. We all have to give him credit because he gives you results.

'The responsibility given to him has made him a better player and a better captain as well. There is so much of competition in IPL, you have got to make decisions pretty quickly. So much of pressure, taking decision at the right time, effecting bowling changes, his demeanour on the field, his body language are pretty calm. At the same time, if he wants to get aggressive, he can. He has that in him to lead any team.'

Rohit's rise as MI captain was also related to the atmosphere surrounding him on and off the field. If it was Gary Kirsten at the start of his international career, it was Duncan Fletcher and then Ravi Shastri who fine-tuned his batting skills and cricketing acumen.

Rohit's marriage to Ritika Sajdeh in December 2015 made him a well-rounded person. Ritika was that missing link that made Rohit a complete person. Nayar said, 'He is pretty outspoken. There have been a lot of misunderstandings (in what he says), but by now people know who he is. He is a fun-loving guy. People know he is pretty blunt. If you ask me or someone

who has known him closely, the biggest change in him as an individual has come because of Ritika.

'Ritika has made the biggest change in terms of his outlook towards life. When Rohit was younger, having a normal conversation other than cricket was difficult for him. Now, he can talk on anything. Ritika has made him into a proper guy, one who can sit with anyone who understands sport and does not understand sport. She has made him well-rounded. They always say, women make the biggest changes, whether for good or bad. In Rohit's case, Ritika has made a great change in him. She is an amazing girl.'

Behind every successful man there stands a woman, as the saying goes. Rohit has been able to concentrate on his cricketing career and leave everything non-cricketing to Ritika, who is also his manager.

Rohit is in the same age group as Mahendra Singh Dhoni, Virat Kohli, Shikhar Dhawan, and Ishan Sharma. Their growth and success have been directly proportional to the growth and success of Indian cricket.

Moreover, Rohit has indeed played a key role in shaping the careers of such superstars as Hardik Pandya and Jaspreet Bumrah in Mumbai Indians. This has been a result of giving them the freedom to do what they want on the cricket field.

Rohit is certainly vocal about certain things in cricket and speaks his heart out, unafraid of the consequences. When the think-tank was still undecided about whether M.S. Dhoni, in his later years and after relinquishing his ODI captaincy in January 2017, should bat at No. 4 or lower down the order, Rohit said that the 2011 World Cup-winning India captain was ideal at No. 4.

As the Indian team was unsettled at No. 4 position, even though Ambati Rayudu was in that slot in the lead up to the 2019 World Cup only to be dropped from the quadrennial event, Rohit said at the start of 2019 that he preferred Dhoni at No. 4. 'Personally, I always feel that Dhoni batting at No. 4 will be ideal for the team but we have got Ambati Rayudu, who has done really well now at No. 4. It totally depends on what the captain and coach think about it. Personally asking, I would be happy if Dhoni bats at four,' said Rohit in January 2019.

In the lead up to the 2019 World Cup, Rohit said that Ambati Rayudu, his trusted middle-order batsman at MI and who also doubles up as an effective wicketkeeper, has solved all the mysteries of No. 4. He added that till the World Cup, there wouldn't be any talk of No. 4.[19]

Rohit is unafraid to voice his opinion on cricketing matters in his capacity as a senior player. Learning the nuances of captaincy in Mumbai Indians, he has brilliantly led India in the times when regular captain Virat Kohli has taken break from the sport.

His success percentage—78.94 per cent in T20Is and 80 per cent in ODIs—has often raised the question of having a split captaincy in Indian cricket, with Kohli leading India in Tests and Rohit in the limited-overs. In comparison, Kohli's respective success percentages are 65.71 per cent and 71.83 per cent.

But as things stand, Rohit will continue to wear the captaincy badge only when Kohli is unavailable. The Board of Control for Cricket in India is not keen on even considering this option as Kohli has emerged as the all-powerful person in Indian cricket.

Like his good friend Nayar said about 'preparation' being the secret mantra to Rohit's success as an IPL captain, his team-

mate Rayudu said Rohit learnt a great deal of leadership from Dhoni.

Rayudu, who was released by MI before 2018 IPL and has since been a key player for CSK, said, 'Dhoni *bhai* has been the captain for all of us including Rohit Sharma and Virat Kohli. Whatever Rohit is becoming, he has learnt from Dhoni as to how Dhoni *bhai* used to captain for India. There won't be much difference and I think he is going in the right direction. Long way to go for him to achieve the success of Dhoni but I am sure he will get there.'[20]

With four IPL titles, Rohit is the most successful captain in the league. Also putting him above other prominent IPL captains is his superior success percentage. His success percentage of 58.65 in the IPL is a shade lower than CSK's Dhoni (59.77 per cent) but far superior to RCB's Kohli (47.16 per cent). Gautam Gambhir, who led KKR to 2 IPL titles (2012 and 2014) has a success percentage of 55.42.

Rohit is among the most-capped players in IPL history. With 188 matches, he is third behind Suresh Raina (193) and Dhoni (190). Having amassed 4,898 runs, Rohit is third behind Kohli (5,412) and Raina (5,368) among the all-time biggest run-getters.

In all these years of the IPL, or even his international cricket, Rohit has rarely been associated with any controversy on the field. Yes, there was one unsavoury incident in the league match against KKR in Kolkata in 2019 when he expressed his disappointment over an umpire's decision. Umpire Nitin Menon adjudged him leg before wicket, which could have gone either way. The ball, upon DRS taken by Rohit, clipped the top corner of the leg-stump and stood as 'Umpire's Call'. A dejected Rohit

knocked the stumps at Menon's end on his way back. He was fined 15 per cent of his match fee for this act.

Rohit has been fined many times for not maintaining his team's over rate, and it has been a regular feature at the Wankhede that matches invariably end close to midnight, if not past it.

One of the most unpopular on-field confrontations in the IPL involved MI and RCB, two bitter rivals who played hard and were captained by two of the most dominant batsmen in modern day cricket, Rohit and Kohli. At the Wankhede in 2014, MI's Kieron Pollard and RCB's Mitchell Starc were involved in a spat, where the bowler first fired a bouncer at Pollard and followed it with a few words.

While just about to deliver the next ball, Pollard withdrew and Starc followed Pollard and hurled the ball in his direction, missing the batsman. In the heat of the moment, Pollard flung his bat at Starc, though the bat fell closer to himself than near the bowler. Pollard's intentions are still debatable.

All along, Rohit, who was going great guns en route to a match-winning 59 not out, was a mute spectator from the non-striker's end. Before he could react, it was all over.

Rohit could have been more proactive in this whole incident. Instead, he stood silent, not taking the initiative that even his rival captain Kohli took when he came to pacify Pollard and was told to not interfere in no uncertain terms by the West Indian. Even when fellow West Indian Chris Gayle from the RCB camp came to calm down Pollard, Rohit seemed to be in his own world.

Rohit has always stayed away from umpires and their decisions and does not interfere much with their decisions. Depending on the game situation, he either tells them politely

A young Rohit Sharma.
Photo credit: Ashutosh Sharma

Coach Dinesh Lad in search of the next Rohit.
Photo credit: Dinesh Lad

Two of India's limited-overs specialists in the last 10 years, Rohit and Suresh Raina.
Photo credit: Ashutosh Sharma

Abhishek Nayar, Rohit's long-time friend and Mumbai Ranji Trophy teammate.
Photo credit: G. Krishnan

Manoj Tiwary, who captained Rohit at India Under-19 level and played with him in ODIs.
Photo credit: G. Krishnan

The bat swing that Sachin Tendulkar talks about.
Photo credit: Ashutosh Sharma

Strong on the on side, his flicks have fetched him many runs.
Photo credit: Ashutosh Sharma

Equally destructive on the off side.
Photo credit: Kamal Sharma

His cover drive is as elegant as anybody's in world cricket.
Photo credit: Ashutosh Sharma

At ease when defending too.
Photo credit: Ashutosh Sharma

His accurate throws often land right on top of the stumps.
Photo credit: Ashutosh Sharma

A souvenir from Sachin Tendulkar's farewell Test against the West Indies in November 2013. Also seen are (L-R) Bhuvneshwar Kumar, Cheteshwar Pujara and umpire Richard Kettleborough.
Photo credit: Ashutosh Sharma

A poignant moment from Tendulkar's last day in Test cricket at Mumbai's Wankhede Stadium.
Photo credit: Ashutosh Sharma

Celebrating his second Test century in Mumbai in the company of No. 11 Mohammad Shami.
Photo credit: Ashutosh Sharma

Lining up with Yuvraj Singh and Zaheer Khan for the national anthem during the 2009 ICC World T20 in England.
Photo credit: Ashutosh Sharma

Making a point during a Test. As a senior member,
he is looked up to by many of his teammates.
Photo credit: Ashutosh Sharma

In a playful mood during the 2019 World Cup.
Photo credit: Kamal Sharma

Rohit and Virat Kohli have a healthy partnership in Tests, averaging 53.56 with three century and three half-century stands in 17 innings.
Photo credit: Ashutosh Sharma

He has filled in as captain of the limited-overs team whenever Virat has taken a break from the rigours of international cricket. Rohit has an impressive record as limited-overs skipper, winning eight out of 10 ODIs and 15 out of 19 T20Is.
Photo credit: Kamal Sharma

All smiles... Flanked by his then team-mate Parthiv Patel and bowling coach Shane Bond, Rohit with one of the IPL trophies after leading his MI team to the third title in 2017.
Photo credit: G. Krishnan

In a jovial mood while addressing the media.
Photo credit: G. Krishnan

With current coach Mahela Jayawardene before the start of 2017 IPL.
Photo credit: G. Krishnan

With coach Ricky Ponting ahead of the 2015 IPL.
Rohit took over as MI captain from Ponting in 2013.
Photo credit: G. Krishnan

Fan following has no age bar. With 87-year-old Charulata Patel after India's win over Bangladesh in the 2019 ICC Cricket World Cup in Birmingham.
Photo credit: Kamal Sharma

With young fan Diya Valeja at a promotional event in Mumbai.
Photo credit: Diya Valeja

National recognition... Receiving the prestigious Arjuna Award from the then Minister of Youth Affairs and Sports, Vijay Goel, in New Delhi on September 16, 2016.
Photo credit: Ministry of Youth Affairs and Sports (GODL-India)

Many awards have come his way like this one, the GQ Sports Personality of the Year 2015.

Life partner... With Ritika Sajdeh at their wedding in Mumbai, December 2015.

that he will press his bowlers to finish overs quickly when they remind him to speed up with the over rate. Otherwise, he just acknowledges them by nodding his head or giving them a simple thumbs up without looking in their direction.

Over the years of regularly officiating his games at the domestic level and in the IPL, umpires vouch that Rohit is not the sort to engage himself in animated conversations with them, as we often see Kohli doing.

As long as he is winning IPL titles, Rohit is a happy captain. He picks his first IPL title (as a player with Deccan Chargers) and the last as captain (in 2019) as his special ones.

In a conversation during the 2020 lockdown, he told his former India team-mate Irfan Pathan and former Aussie pacer Brett Lee, 'The first one with Deccan Chargers, which was 11 years ago, way back in 2009 in SA, was very special. It was my first IPL title. We know how challenging it was to win with that team.

'The second one was last year. The reason I say it is because my little daughter (Samaira) was there in the stands watching me play from day one to the last game. I was keeping my fingers crossed if she could sit the entire game but she did that for the entire tournament. After winning the championship, she came to the ground as well with me. That was special for me as well.'[21]

EIGHT

Stooping to Conquer

Less than a week after Sachin scored his long-awaited 100th international century in March 2012, a felicitation was held by industrialist and Mumbai Indians owner Mukesh Ambani. At the event, Tendulkar nominated Rohit and Kohli to emulate his feat. Bollywood superstar Salman Khan commented, 'Sachin *ke record thodna mushkil hi nahin, namumkin hain* (Sachin's record is not only difficult to break but also impossible).'

Curious to know if he thought anyone could break his record of hundred hundreds, Salman asked Tendulkar, 'Can anyone break your record?'

Tendulkar then stood up and said, 'They are sitting in this room, our youngsters. I can see them. Virat and Rohit are the ones. As long as any Indian breaks, I don't mind,' he said.[22]

Rohit was into his fifth year in international cricket at the time. He had not yet made his Test debut and scored only two international centuries, both in ODIs. He had 98 more to go.

At the same time, Virat, in his fourth year in Team India colours, had notched up 12 international centuries, one in Tests

and 11 in ODIs. That meant he had 88 more to go to live up to Tendulkar's expectations.

Such was Rohit's talent and ability. He had only himself to blame for not fulfilling his potential, especially in Tests. For a batsman who can score not one, not two, but three double centuries in ODIs, who can score five centuries in a single edition of the World Cup, who has scored four hundreds in T20Is, the format in which Kohli does not have even one, Rohit has just not been able to bring that form to Tests and has been an underachiever in that format.

Rohit had his share of injuries of course, but that should not be given as an excuse for not realising his full potential.

That said, none could be like Tendulkar, carrying a billion dreams on his shoulders and living up to everyone's expectations. In that same felicitation, former India captain and legendary opening batsman Sunil Gavaskar paid glowing tribute to Tendulkar, saying, 'The time I thought Sachin would really go on to get these hundred hundreds or more hundreds was when he got that hundred in Perth' (114 in the fifth and final Test of the 1991–1992 tour of Australia, a knock that Tendulkar himself rates as his best knock). 'He made it look so simple, he was on top of everything, his balance was fantastic. It is the balance on the field and off the field which is why he is in this position today,' Gavaskar told an elite gathering of Indian cricket team members, Bollywood stars and others.

That century in Perth was Tendulkar's third in Tests. He did not score an ODI century until 1994. India did not play their first T20I until December 2006 in South Africa, which was Tendulkar's first and last.

Now established as a leading batsman in world cricket today, Rohit has earned a name for himself in limited overs cricket and in the course of time has scored a total of 39 international centuries—six in Tests, twenty-nine in ODIs and four in T20Is. He is still 61 short of Tendulkar's prediction.

On the other hand, Kohli has grown into one of the top batsmen in all formats and seems to score centuries at will and double centuries in Test matches at the drop of a hat. He is well on his way to achieving what his idol Tendulkar expected of him. Kohli has 70 centuries—27 in Tests and 43 in ODIs—in international cricket and needs 30 more for the milestone.

At 31 years, and with a good number of matches ahead of him, Kohli stands a bright chance to score the hundred hundreds.

One of Kohli's good friends, Kevin Pietersen, the controversial former England batsman and captain, was asked if Kohli could go on to break Tendulkar's hundred hundreds. He said, 'It's difficult because of injury and the longevity of Tendulkar's career. Tendulkar wasn't as emotional when he was in the field and he did not carry the same sort of aggressive attitude on the field. He was a lot more relaxed. It depends on how long Virat Kohli continues to play.

'Remember, Kohli plays all three forms of the game, plus he plays the IPL. For majority of Sachin Tendulkar's career, there was no T20 cricket and there was no IPL. So it all depends on how long Kohli plays for.'[23]

That rules Rohit out of contention for the hundred hundreds but does not take away his greatness or the achievements he has had in international cricket, especially in the last three years, smashing in excess of 1,000 runs in ODIs in 2017, 2018 and 2019, collecting 19 centuries in the process.

Add to that three T20I hundreds and three more in Tests, and you find that Rohit has had a remarkable three years.

It is definitely his heavyweight performance in ODIs and T20Is that has given him a new lease of life in Tests in 2019.

Rohit ushered in the year 2019 with the news of the birth of his daughter Samaira, born on 30 December 2018, the fifth day of the Boxing Day Test in which he scored 63 in the first innings. He missed the fourth and final Test, the New Year's Test in Sydney, to fly home to see his new-born.

Rohit returned to Australia well in time for the ODIs and scored 133 in his first knock, though it ended up on the losing side. He had to take control of the innings as India lost three wickets with only four runs on the board. Rohit and Dhoni tried to repair the damage with a 137-run partnership for the fourth wicket after Australian pacers Jhye Richardson and Jason Behrendorff.

Another effective stand was what India required, but Rohit did not get that. He eventually fell in the 46th over as India ended 34 runs short of Australia's 288/5.

Having led Mumbai Indians to an unmatched fourth IPL title in 2019, Rohit lived up to his own promise of opening in the entire IPL season ahead of the ICC Cricket World Cup. He did have a reasonable outing, hitting two fifties while accumulating 405 runs at a modest average of under 30. But playing the new ball and in the powerplay mattered most to Rohit as well as getting enough practice ahead of the quadrennial event.

The 2019 World Cup in England and Wales was Rohit's second. His first was four years earlier in Australia and New Zealand, where he scored one century against Bangladesh,

137, and two fifties to finish the tournament with a handsome average of 47.14.

Little did Rohit know that he would end up as the highest run getter in the 12th edition of the global event—648 runs at 81.00, one run more than Australia's David Warner (647 runs at 71.88 in one more innings). Neither did he know that he would end up with five hundreds in a single tournament. Never before has this been done in a World Cup. Rohit believed in taking one game at a time, in not looking too far ahead than what was at hand.

Rohit had forgettable warm-up matches against Bangladesh and New Zealand, notching up only 17 and 2, respectively.

But Rohit is a big-stage player who believes in getting into his rhythm. He has never been one to go on the offensive from the first ball. His style of batting has, of late, consisted of watching the initial few deliveries, understanding how the pitch behaves, how the ball behaves, and after assessing the conditions, getting down to play his long innings.

He also mentally calculated the World Cup scoring trend. When India played their first match on the seventh day into the tournament, their first opponent South Africa and four other teams—England, Sri Lanka, Afghanistan and Pakistan—had already finished with two matches each.

It was a scratchy start to his World Cup campaign in Southampton. He was dropped on 1 and again on 107, both off Kagiso Rabada. But batting is about making the most of opportunities. Rohit remained unbeaten on 122 and ensured India crossed the line with six wickets in hand. He walked away with the 'Man of the Match' award. In the process, he moved

past Sourav Ganguly's tally of 22 ODI hundreds to lie third behind Tendulkar and Kohli.

At the end of that match-winning knock against the Proteas, Rohit admitted it was not a typical Rohit Sharma innings. He said, 'There was something in it for the bowlers through the game. I couldn't play my natural game. I had to take my time to play shots, had to cut down certain shots I love to play. Wanted to leave a lot of balls initially, was trying to stick to the basics and build partnerships even though it was a small total (227/9). All the batsmen in the team have a job, it's their role to bat through and get the job done. We can't rely on one or two individuals. That's been the hallmark of this team. We've done that well, this is a big tournament and at some stage someone else will put their hand up and do the job for us. We're playing a little early in the summer in England, weather was good through the day, you don't sweat. I had fun, wasn't typical Rohit Sharma innings, had to play out the overs to ensure I get the job done.'[24]

In the second match, it was his opening partner Shikhar Dhawan's turn to collect the 'Man of the Match' award for his knock of 117.

The Rohit–Shikhar opening partnership developed as one of the most fearsome combinations in limited overs cricket since they began to open together from the 2013 Champions Trophy. The right hand–left hand combination at the top posed problems to the opposition right from the word go. They developed a perfect understanding between themselves that extended beyond the field and into their families. Their wives are close friends and Dhawan's children can just about do anything with Rohit for fun on tours.

The understanding between them has worked well for the country. If one is on the offensive, the other complements him by playing a watchful knock. In recent times, it is Rohit who does not mind playing second fiddle to Shikhar so as to be able to play as many overs as possible. The longer the tenure Rohit has at the crease, the bigger is his score and greater are the chances of India winning.

After the win against South Africa, India ran into defending champions Australia at the Oval. The 127-run opening stand between Rohit and Dhawan, with the former falling for 57, laid the foundation for India posting their highest World Cup total against Australia and their fourth highest in the mega event—352/5.

The target was too much for the asking, even by Aussie standards, as they had to contend with India's bowling heroes Bhuvneshwar Kumar, Jasprit Bumrah and Yuzvendra Chahal, who shared the responsibility to power India to a 36-run victory.

In this match, Rohit became the fastest Indian in terms of innings (37) to reach 2,000 ODI runs against a single team, faster than even the likes of Sachin Tendulkar (40 innings against Australia), Virat Kohli (44 against Sri Lanka) and Viv Richards (44 against Australia).

It was also in this match that the Rohit–Dhawan combination ended for the rest of the tournament as the left-hander was hit by Pat Cummins, fractured his thumb and was ruled out.

The onus was on Rohit at the top of the order, even though he had the capable and immensely talented K.L. Rahul to open the batting with. Playing in his first World Cup, Rahul had been around for four years in the international scene, doing his best to become a regular feature in all the formats, though he was in

the 'Man of the Match' awards in both. The comfortable 28-run win helped India qualify for the semi-finals with a game to spare.

Based on how he flayed the Bangladesh attack at Edgbaston, Birmingham, talks of Rohit having a bright chance of scoring a double century were doing the rounds. Rohit and Rahul shared 180 for the first wicket in under 30 overs, showing signs of bigger things to come. Captain Kohli had only admiration for Rohit's knock when he said at the presentation, 'I have been watching it for years now. He's the best one-day player around and we are so delighted to see him. When he plays like that, everybody is happy to see him strike this so well.'

As for scoring his fourth century of the tournament, Rohit said, 'Oh I thought I just got a hundred today. My mantra is whatever has happened in the past is in the past. Those in form have to bat long and get the team to a big score. I need to focus on the next game now.'

Focus he did on the next game to score his third consecutive century and fifth of the World Cup, surpassing Kumar Sangakkara's record of four scored in the 2015 edition. Like in the previous two games, Rohit fell soon after reaching his century. For the second successive match, Rohit and Rahul shared 180 or more, going nine runs better than their previous stand. Once again, it was Rohit who fell first.

Not one to play for records, Rohit admitted at the post-match presentation, 'I wasn't thinking about milestones, my job is to keep my head straight and get the team towards the finishing line. When you are in, shot selection becomes very important, I try to calculate how I want to go forward, and it has paid dividends. You have to be disciplined in batting, and I've learned from my mistakes in the past.'

Rohit would have bargained each of his centuries for the World Cup. While he had a glorious tournament personally, India's campaign ended with the semi-final defeat to New Zealand in Manchester. How true were Sourav Ganguly's words when he said after Rohit's century against Sri Lanka, his fifth of the tournament! 'I just hope Rohit has kept a hundred or two in the reserve, for the semi-final and, hopefully, the final as well,' Ganguly said.[25]

On his part, Rohit said after India's last league match, 'I'm not here for records. I'm here to play cricket. I'm here to play and score runs and lift the cup. That is what I'm here for. I'm not looking at all those things at all, honestly. For us, as cricketers, it's important to get the job done, because we all have been looking forward to this World Cup, which comes every four years. You have to wait four years for this. Eventually the job for us is to go and win the semi-finals and the final before that. But as long as that is not accomplished, no matter how many runs you score in the tournament or how many hundreds you get, you won't feel satisfied.'

As it turned out, India could not gather themselves against New Zealand in the semi-final, losing Rohit, Rahul and Kohli for one each against the disciplined Matt Henry and Trent Boult, leaving India precariously placed at 5/3 chasing the Kiwis' 239/8. Dhoni, who struggled for his 50, could not finish the crucial game for India, shutting the doors on an otherwise dominating campaign.

Rohit equalled Tendulkar's record for most World Cup centuries, six, and ended the calendar year 2019 with 10 runs short of 1,500 to be named Wisden's ODI Cricketer of the Year. The year ended in the same way as it started for him—with a

lot of runs. He notched up a century in the penultimate innings of the year—159 against the West Indies in Visakhapatnam—before scoring 63 in Cuttack in his last ODI knock of 2019.

But the rest of 2019 post World Cup was about his performances in Tests. He was brought in to open for the first time in Tests in Visakhapatnam against South Africa after playing in the middle and lower middle-order in his first 27 Tests. A new opening pair was formed with the improving Mayank Agarwal. Rohit straightaway scored a century in each of the two innings.

Rohit was in the squad for the two Tests in the West Indies in August, India's first Tests in the World Test Championship cycle, but he did not figure in the playing XI, as it was a settled unit with Rahul opening with Agarwal and Hanuma Vihari filling the No. 6 slot after a packed middle-order comprising Pujara, Kohli and Rahane.

However, India could not keep Rohit out of the Tests for long as they also needed a solid batsman at the top of the order, and none fitted the bill better than Rohit. Captain Kohli threw his weight behind Rohit to open in Tests, at least on home soil when South Africa came calling for three Tests and followed by Bangladesh for two.

'If he succeeds in the opening role, then our batting order at the top becomes more lethal. It is difficult to have a player like that to not start every time,' Kohli said on the eve of the first Test in Visakhapatnam. 'If he comes into his own, then the whole batting order looks a completely different batting order anywhere in the world.'

Rohit followed his first innings of 176—one short of the 177 he scored in his maiden Test innings against the West Indies in Kolkata in Tendulkar's farewell series in November 2013—with

127 in the second as India trounced South Africa by 203 runs. Undoubtedly, Rohit was 'Man of the Match'. He was initially watchful, leaving well outside the off stump before playing the cut shots and using his feet to the spinners to slam five sixes on the opening day.

Along with Agarwal, who became the fourth Indian after Dilip Sardesai, Vinod Kambli and Karun Nair to convert his maiden Test hundred into a double century, Rohit shared 317 for the opening wicket in the first innings. This was the highest opening stand for India vs South Africa Tests, and the third instance of an Indian opening pair sharing 300 or more in Tests.

Rohit was struck with the reality of opening in Test cricket in the second match in Pune, where he was done in by a Kagiso Rabada length delivery that nicked him behind for 14. In the third Test in Ranchi, he was back to his own self scoring a big hundred.

On 20 October, Rohit added to his three ODI double centuries with a maiden Test double ton, 212, reaching the milestone with a pulled six to mid-wicket off Rabada. It was the second day of the Ranchi Test and Virender Sehwag's birthday. How proud Sehwag would have felt as he played fearlessly and was unafraid to go for a six when approaching a century, double century or even triple century!

Rohit was candid at the end of the second day's play in Ranchi when talking about opening in Tests and his double century. He said, 'I don't think about records' (Rohit became the fourth batsman in history to score a Test and an ODI double ton after Tendulkar, Sehwag and the West Indian Chris Gayle). 'When you are batting, you are not aware of what all's happening, what records are being broken and which ones are

going to be broken. I will look back at all the records once I stop playing, not now.'[26]

Reflecting on his Test double century, Rohit said, 'It was the most challenging. I haven't played much (Tests), only 30. So, yes, in terms of what was thrown at me in this particular Test, it was the most challenging one.'

Rohit also said that opening in Tests and opening in limited overs were entirely different.

'Whenever I was playing, I wanted to do well. Not that only after opening in Tests did I want to do well. I have been opening in limited overs. The challenges are different while opening in Tests. I know it is challenging. I have only played in three Tests as an opener. I have a long way to go. Am not reading too much in these three Tests. I will take the positives.'

Speaking of the challenges of opening in Tests, Rohit said, 'It is about how you prepare yourself, what you talk to yourself, what you want to go out there and achieve. Playing the first ball of a Test as against going out to bat in the 30th or 40th over is a different ballgame. Of course, there is nothing different in terms of technique. I know the basics of the game, what you need to do as an opener in whichever format you bat, the new ball does something. In Ranchi and Pune (Tests where he opened), the ball did quite a bit than even in overseas conditions like in Australia. With the new ball, wherever you play, you have to have some sort of understanding of the basics of the game, which ones to play at, which ones you want to leave.'

Rohit bagged the 'Man of the Match' award in the third Test as well as the Man of the Series.

Captain Kohli was pleased with Rohit opening in the series against South Africa. After the 3–0 drubbing of the Proteas in

Ranchi, he said, 'The way he has batted, even after we have missed a session or two–three hours of play, his batting pace has given the team enough time to bowl the other team out twice. Credit goes entirely to the player. The way he has overcome his anxiety of what the challenges could be opening in Tests has been incredible. He has been one of the best openers in ODIs for some time. To win Man of the Series award in his first series as an opener has been a top performance from him.'[27]

Rohit may have settled down as an opener in Tests quite easily, amassing 529 runs at 132.25 with three centuries. He was almost 200 runs ahead of the second highest run getter in the series, his opening partner Agarwal, who scored 215 and 108 in the first and second Tests, respectively.

In the next Test series however, played at home against Bangladesh, Rohit could not survive the shining new ball. He went for an expansive shot and edged behind in the first Test in Indore and fell for six. In the second Test, which was India's first ever day-night Test, he shouldered arms to be trapped leg before. This was at his favourite venue, Kolkata, and he fell for 21.

His opening partner Agarwal was unstoppable and played his career best of 243 in Indore. His score was the fifth highest individual score by an Indian opener in Tests—Sehwag owns the first four (319, 309, 293 and 254).

Rohit is aware that it will be a different cup of tea when he opens in foreign conditions. He missed that when India toured New Zealand for two Tests earlier in 2020 as he was ruled out after sustaining left calf muscle strain during the fifth T20Is preceding the Tests. India had a tough series, losing both in Wellington and Christchurch. It was a tour in which India won

the first five internationals—all five T20Is 5–0—and lost the next five internationals, three ODIs 0–3 and two Tests, 0–2.

He is also aware of the difficulty of opening the Tests in Australia, where India are slated to tour this year end in their quest to retain the Border–Gavaskar Trophy that was won on their soil for the first time in their previous trip in 2018–2019.

Rohit expressed his displeasure at the prospect of facing Aussie pacer Josh Hazlewood in particular. Talking to his former India team-mate Irfan Pathan and retired Aussie quick Brett Lee on a video chat during the lockdown, Rohit said, 'Someone I don't want to face in Test cricket would be Josh Hazlewood. I know for a fact that when I come to Australia for the Test matches, I have to be prepared mentally to be disciplined against him. This guy is going to hit the length every now and then. You have to decide which balls to leave, which ones to hit and wait till whenever he gives you the loose ball to try and score runs of.'[28]

Rohit will do well to adopt the legendary Gavaskar's principle of 'giving the first half hour to the bowlers and rest of the day is yours'. This will be required especially when he tours overseas.

Though form deserted him against Bangladesh in Tests, he was in his usual self in the limited overs until the lockdown. It did not matter to him if he had Dhawan to open with or the improved, hard-working Rahul; Rohit went about his business as usual, with the profound confidence of having succeeded as a Test opener too.

Now an opener in all the three formats, Rohit has got the security and won the faith of his captain in Tests too. His place in limited overs is secured, no doubt about it.

India ended the year 2019 and began 2020 with three pairs of openers in the limited-overs—Rohit and Dhawan, Dhawan and Rahul, and Rohit and Rahul, as either Rohit or Dhawan was injured or resting and not available.

Rohit also led India to triumph in the T20I series against Bangladesh as regular skipper Kohli took a break from international cricket in consultation with the selectors led my M.S.K. Prasad. He also led in the fifth T20I in New Zealand as Kohli rested after India had already won the series and gave the highly skilled Sanju Samson a chance.

Rohit also got his share of break-time from international cricket when Sri Lanka visited India in January 2020 for three stand-alone T20Is. Sri Lanka replaced the originally scheduled Zimbabwe, who were suspended by the ICC.

Rohit's return for the ODIs against Australia after the break presented the team management with the headache of whom to drop between Dhawan and Rahul. As it turned out, Rohit and Dhawan opened while Rahul batted at one drop in Mumbai, No. 5 in the second in Rajkot. Rahul opened in the third and deciding one in Bengaluru after Dhawan injured his shoulder while fielding, not to bat in the run-chase.

As it turned out, Rohit was majestic in the Bengaluru ODI, scoring 109 and anchoring the innings before going on the offensive and putting India on the path to a seven-wicket win.

It was his last ODI knock, and he played his last two T20I knocks before the world went into a lockdown due to COVID-19 and all sporting activity came to a standstill for at least four months.

NINE

Forging Friendships

On the eve of the 2006–2007 much-anticipated high-profile Ranji Trophy final between Mumbai and Bengal at the Wankhede, former India captain and currently head coach of the team Ravi Shastri predicted that two young guns, one from either side, would be the ones to watch in the future. 'Watch out for Rohit Sharma and Manoj Tiwary, they are going to the stars of the future,' Shastri said on the phone to a journalist of a national daily.

That Ranji Trophy final had all the superstars of the Indian team. For starters, Sachin Tendulkar played in that match. Wasim Jaffer, Zaheer Khan, Ajit Agarkar and Ramesh Powar also made up the Mumbai team, led by the domestic giant Amol Muzumdar.

Sourav Ganguly filled the Bengal line-up. The Bengal team also had Rohan Gavaskar, Laxmi Ratan Shukla, Ranadeb Bose and was captained by Deep Dasgupta, who had by then kept wickets for the country in eight Tests and five ODIs.

Rohit and Manoj did show glimpses of what they had that made the 'champion of champions' Shastri predict confidently

that they were the future stars of Indian cricket. While Manoj had a more successful outing than Rohit with 42 and 94, the Mumbaikar had a more impactful knock in the second innings, when he made 57 to make up for his first innings' 14.

Manoj stood as a thorn in the Mumbai bowling flesh in the second innings and played a magnificent knock before throwing it away, playing away from his body and giving his nemesis Rohit a catch at point off Abhishek Nayar six shy of a century.

That match, though, will be remembered for Tendulkar's masterly 105, a typical knock from the batting genius from whose blade a century is almost a given whenever he plays for Mumbai in Ranji Trophy in between his international schedules.

Ganguly, by then a former India captain, flopped in the first innings but scored a fighting 90 in the second. But Bengal's collective failure in the first innings (143 in reply to Mumbai's 320) saw them lose the game then and there. Mumbai eventually won by 132 runs for their 37th Ranji trophy title.

While Rohit has climbed the international ladder, Manoj did get his chance there months after this epic Ranji Trophy final. But fate was cruel to him. On the eve of an ODI in Bangladesh in May 2007 where he was certain to make his debut, Manoj hurt his right shoulder during practice and was ruled out. He had to wait until February 2008, when he was flown to Australia and presented with his ODI cap within hours of reaching, only to be bowled by a lethal Brett Lee yorker for two.

The then India captain Rahul 'The Wall' Dravid also saw a bright future for the talented Manoj. 'I am sure we will see a lot of him in the near future I am sure he will get through the phase and make a comeback very quickly,' Dravid said while announcing that Manoj was ruled out of the three-match ODI

series in Bangladesh. 'It's sad for a young kid who has come to play his first match to get such an unfortunate injury. But to look at it positively, he is very young and has a lot of cricket ahead of him.'

Reflecting on what went right for Rohit that did not go well for Manoj, the Bengal right-handed batsman said, 'Injury to me was a major blow in Bangladesh before making my ODI debut there. At that point of time, I was playing really well, was in a very good flow. I had a lot of runs. Confidence was pretty high, untimely injury took me back by one year.'

Speaking about Rohit, Manoj said, 'As far as Rohit is concerned, he was always talented and naturally gifted. During the U-19 days, when I was leading East Zone. In one of the zonal games at Bangalore's M. Chinnaswamy Stadium against West, there was this young guy I have never heard of before. That was the first time I saw Rohit play. In no time he scored a hundred. For an opposition captain, it was difficult to set field for him. Having led U-16, U-19 sides, I had a fair idea of captaincy. But, I was finding it very difficult to place field for Rohit. And the bowlers were unable to contain him.'

Manoj observed some rare qualities in Rohit's batting that have stayed with him.

'To hit a good ball for four, whatever I have observed of him and others, he had a natural ability to hit good balls for four. From one spot, he could hit in three or four areas. After that, his desire, his work ethics, his natural ability and the kind of innings he played in front of my eyes made me fall in love with his batting.'

Rohit's positive body language, even after a failure, was another feature that Manoj admired in him.

'Not many associate him with fearless batting. He is a carefree kind of personality. He will not sulk after a bad performance. It will not be evident in his body language. Even if he fails in a couple of innings, he does not show it. That has eventually helped him. There are so many players, in healthy competition throughout India, if you are worried about past performances, you will not eventually stay in the present. Rohit was different from the rest. He knew how to deal with his failures. That has helped in his batting a lot. He was approaching new games with fresh mind. There was no baggage whatsoever.'

Rohit's confident personality rubbed off on his game as well. He is unafraid to take on any bowler in the world and treats even the deadliest of them with scant respect, making subtle changes to his batting as his career progressed.

Asked if he has seen any change in Rohit over the years, Manoj said, 'The change has come for the better. There was a phase when he was not scoring runs. I think he identified what were the reasons behind it and he worked on it on and off the field. By on the field, I mean his skill sets, temperament. And off the field, there are so many things that disturb a player's mindset. He has worked on them as well. What I observed was that he changed for the better and that eventually showed in his performance. There was a brief period when he was getting very frustrated. I think the management at that point of time has to be credited. They backed him. You know now Rohit Sharma as a world-class player, someone scoring five hundreds in a single World Cup. That's unimaginable.

'His batting is pleasing to the eye, so effortless and brings smiles on people's faces. Talent and hard-work go side-by-side.

When hard work is mixed with talent, he becomes an atomic bomb. He can hit the ball a long, long way.'

When two contemporaries who set out on a similar path divert along their ways due to circumstances beyond their control, the one who missed out is bound to feel jealous of the other. That is only human nature. But Manoj says, 'There was no jealousy, absolutely not. I have been raised and told that if I had to do well, I had to do better than the other guy. I always looked to contribute. That's how I played my cricket. I felt good for Rohit. I have seen him from close quarters. He has a pure heart. He is a good soul. If that good soul scores runs even if you are competing with him, I feel happy.

'It's eventually about grabbing opportunities, and I am a firm believer in destiny. We both could have played together even till now. You never know. When I played for India, he was in the team. After my ODI hundred (104 not out against the West Indies in Chennai, December 2011), I found no place in the playing XI in the next 14 games. That had made a little full stop in my international career.

'After that hundred, I got more confidence. Before that game, I have always questioned myself if I belonged in international cricket. That hundred and "Man of the Match" performance for India gave me a lot of confidence, that made me realise that I belonged in international cricket. But not getting a game for 14 matches after the 100 broke my confidence. If someone is in good flow, is in good rhythm, you want to give that individual enough chances rather than make him sit outside the playing XI. If the communication is not well, it becomes difficult. That happened in my case.

'Keeping my story aside, I'm very happy with the way Rohit is performing, the way he is leading in IPL, captaining India. It's great to see your fellow team-mate, whom you have known closely, do well. You feel good about it. At the end of the day, if someone whom you know is making millions happy by virtue of batting, it gives me immense satisfaction.'

Manoj ended up playing only twelve ODIs and three T20Is for the country. Besides that 104 not out, Manoj played another significant knock for India against Sri Lanka in Pallekele in August 2012. His 65 came at a crucial time when India were 87 for three. He shared a 110-run stand with Gautam Gambhir for the fourth wicket as India went on to put up 294/7, eventually winning by 20 runs.

If Manoj has seen Rohit as an India U-19 team-mate and India team-mate as well as his opponent in domestic competitions, Abhishek Nayar, left-handed batsman and right-arm medium-pacer for Mumbai and India, has been close to him for nearly two decades.

Nayar, now a mentor and spots talent for Kolkata Knight Riders, has been close friends with Rohit since their teen years. 'He was 15 or 16 years when I met Rohit for the first time. He had come to play Moin-ud-Dowlah Trophy. He was my room-mate. We became close friends when we started playing Ranji Trophy together,' said Nayar.

Sharing a room with Rohit was fun. In fact, spending time with Rohit is great fun, as he constantly cracks jokes, which come naturally to the 'Hitman'. Rohit is a well-known prankster with his team-mates. In two of the three ODIs that Nayar played, he shared the dressing room with Rohit in the West Indies in June 2009. Nayar said, 'Rohit is crazy fun. It's been a while since I

spent time in the dressing room with him. He is someone you can sit all day long with and be entertained. He is so likeable. The crazy thing is he is not trying to be funny, he is not trying to crack a joke. It comes naturally to him. His mannerisms are such that the way he talks is funny. Even in press conferences, it is not that he is trying to be funny. He says so innocently that it becomes funny. We have had some outstanding times. Even now when we meet and discuss about the fun in the Mumbai dressing room. It has been unbelievable. There have been some really tough times but he is cracking jokes, not bothered about the situation. He is keeping the atmosphere light. It was so easy when he was there. Amazing.

'You can rely on Rohit to say something that will calm the situation down. If you are under pressure, he is the guy you would want to go and sit next to, and you will feel better. He is so carefree and doesn't show pressure that even you start feeling so good about yourself. In general, you spend time with a confident person, it rubs on your outlook. That's what Rohit did.'

Nayar, about three-and-a-half years older than Rohit, narrates an incident from an otherwise very tense Mumbai dressing room.

'We were playing a Ranji Trophy semi-final match, Mumbai versus Baroda in Vadodara (2006–07). In the second innings we were 0/5 (five wickets down without a run on the board). After five wickets down, I went into bat, scored 10 and got out. We were 17/6. I came in and sat in the dressing room.

'Rohit was on a different zone of cracking jokes. We all are laughing. Our coach, Pravin sir (Amre), sitting behind us was like, "*Arre, team ka score dekho aur tum logon ka kya chal raha*

hai? Tum kya kar raho?" ("Look at the team score and what's happening with you guys. What are you doing?") Rohit was joking non-stop. This guy was like "enjoy".

'Why it is so fresh in my mind is that it is so easy for everyone to keep a tense mood in the dressing room thinking about losing from 0/5 and 17/6. And, this guy was in a different rant, at a different level after scoring 6 in the first innings and a first-ball zero in the second. He was so chilled-out and said others should also chill, not break head. We ended up winning that match. His keeping the dressing room lively was part of making sure pressure was not felt.'

As it turned out, Mumbai, with a 91-run first innings lead, recovered from the blows of Baroda's new bowlers Irfan Pathan and Rakesh Patel that reduced them to 17/6 to make 145 and set Baroda a target of 237. The never-say-die Mumbai wicket-keeper Vinayak Samant bailed Mumbai out of the woods to make 66 and shared 66 with all-rounder Wilkin Mota (33) to save the multiple-time Ranji champions from embarrassment. It was the match before the final against Bengal that they went on to win, and Rohit was earmarked along with Manoj as one to watch for in the future.

Nayar's own contribution in that 63-run Mumbai win in Vadodara was 3/38 as Baroda were bowled out for 173.

Manoj agreed with Rohit's ability to keep the dressing room alive even in pressure situations. He said, 'He has always been a fun-loving guy. He does a lot of pranks with players with whom he is very close with. He has always been on the lookout to give it a go as far as jokes and pulling someone's legs are concerned. He wants to be a lively character. His nature is such that once he is comfortable with a few individuals, he starts opening up. He

is a very good soul. He has got a pure heart. He is very generous as well. That's what I like about him. Even though I had some healthy competition with him for the Indian team, I have always liked him. I like him and admire him.'

Nayar played in three ODIs, but he is known more for his gutsy performances for Mumbai as well as for his awkward stance, legs wide apart and almost falling over. After finishing with Mumbai and with the intention of not blocking a youngster from getting into the Mumbai squad, Nayar played one season (2018–2019) for Puducherry before calling it quits.

Nayar sees the same Rohit today as he did when he met him for the first time. Nayar said, 'Rohit then was exactly the same who he is today. He was a very funny, witty guy. He did not bother too much about the world. He was carefree, liked to do what he felt like doing. He was someone who liked to bat a lot. He was not very big on training. One that stood out for me about Rohit always was he had a lot of self-belief in his abilities and what he can do on the cricket.'

Nayar said Rohit always had that self-belief in him. 'Any changes in Rohit from then and now is his approach to life, the way he speaks, how he approaches people. All these changes for the good are because of his wife Ritika,' he said. He added, 'In terms of cricket, I see the same mannerisms in Rohit that I saw in him first. Yes, there are changes in his skills, how he plays bowlers, they are natural growth. There was insecurity in trying to prove himself. That has gone out of the window. Now he is a very secure individual, he knows he is the king. That's the only change, which comes with time. At that point of time, he always believed that his cricket was supreme.'

When asked where the belief to excel came from for Rohit, Nayar said, 'Belief is a mannerism. It doesn't come from anything. For a lot of people who possess self-belief, it's a natural skill you acquire, something you can build on. Rohit had tough circumstances growing up. The ability to zone in when a game comes is something he had from the inception. There were times when you look from outside that he would not score runs, but once he went in, he would completely zone in and score runs. Rohit stands out.'

Nayar credited coach Dinesh Lad for providing Rohit with the necessary support in his formative years. He said, 'Rohit had this love for the game, yes. There was Dinesh Lad, who was very supportive of him, helped him overcome tough times by giving a platform to play cricket, He had a support system in his coach. He was always the kind of the guy who was a survivor. He would play tennis ball cricket to make money. From the U-14 days, people knew what he was capable of. He was not an unknown commodity or came out of the blue. He was special. That was something that was there with him always. What has happened over the years is basically the diamond has been polished and made ready.'

Asked what trait in Rohit he admired the most, Nayar said, 'For me the most special quality I had seen in him and still admire right now is that Rohit has not changed at all. This guy is the same. Rohit Sharma before playing for India and Rohit Sharma playing today is the same with friends, is the same amongst people. He says what he wants to say, he is a happy-go-lucky guy. It's amazing how he maintains balance. I can see a lot of people losing that balance. Rohit has been the same. That, for

me, is the greatest quality and the greatest strength. That is why he is succeeding every single time.'

Rohit is known for his knack for hitting sixes almost at will. He holds the world record for most sixes in a Test match, 13, which he scored against South Africa in his first Test as an opener in October 2019 in Visakhapatnam. He scored five of them on the first day of the Test, using his feet jolly well to deposit the Proteas spinners in the stands. In his first innings score of 176, Rohit had half-a-dozen sixes, and in the second knock, when he scored 127, he had seven of them.

His 13 maximum hits was one better than Wasim Akram's 12, which came against Zimbabwe in Sheikhupura, where he scored 257 not out. Till date, this is the highest score by a batsman at No. 8.

Furthermore, Rohit has the record for most sixes hit in a Test series—19—against South Africa in 2019–2020, four better than West Indies' Shimron Hetmeyer (15, against Bangladesh in 2018).

In 32 Tests, Rohit has smashed 52 sixes. This means he hits 1.625 sixes in one Test, or 162.5 sixes for every 100 Tests played. Some of the big-hitters of the game who top the sixes charts in Tests fall well below Rohit in terms of the average sixes hit per Test.

No. 1 in the list, New Zealander Brendon McCullum, who has played in 101 Tests, has hit 107 sixes. This converts to 105.9 sixes for every 100 Tests played. Among others, Australia's Adam Gilchrist has 104.2 sixes per 100 Tests; West Indies' Chris Gayle, 97 sixes per 100 Tests; India's own Virender Sehwag, 87.5 per 100 Tests. Someone who comes close to Rohit is the disgraced

New Zealander Chris Cairns, who hit 140.3 sixes in every 100 Tests.

It is no surprise that Rohit tops the list for most sixes in T20 International career—127 in 108 matches, eight clear of second-placed Martin Guptill of New Zealand. The closest Indian in this list is Virat Kohli (76 sixes in 96 matches).

In ODIs, Rohit is topmost among those still actively playing with 244 sixes in 224 matches. He is fourth in the list of most career sixes, only behind the retired Shahid Afridi of Pakistan (351 sixes in 369 ODIs), Chris Gayle of the West Indies (331 sixes in 301 ODIs) and Sri Lanka's Sanath Jayasuriya (270 sixes in 445 ODIs).

On an average, Rohit hits 112.442 sixes for every 100 innings batted in ODIs, which is far better than Afridi (95.122 sixes for every 100 ODI innings batted) and Jayasuriya (62.36 sixes for every 100 innings) but marginally less than Gayle (112.58 sixes for every 100 innings).

In his entire international career, Rohit has smashed 423 sixes, which is the third highest, behind Gayle (534) and Afridi (476). Furthermore, he is the fastest to have hit 400 international sixes, getting there in his 354th international appearance, during the third T20I in Mumbai against the West Indies in December 2019. Rohit is also the only player to hit at least 10 sixes in an international innings in each of the three formats. He smashed 10 sixes off 35 balls en route to scoring the joint-fastest T20I hundred, sharing the record with South Africa's David Miller.

Rohit's six-hitting abilities have only improved with age, like wine. From the time he turned 30 on 30 April 2017, Rohit has hit 230 international sixes—27 in Tests, 127 in ODIs and 76 in T20Is. And at 33, with the prime of his batting still ahead of

him, one can expect Rohit to only go big and toy with bowlers the world over.

It may come as a surprise that Rohit has only 194 sixes in his 188-match IPL career. He is joint fourth in the all-time list for most IPL sixes with Suresh Raina, and second Indian behind Mahendra Singh Dhoni, who has 209. Gayle and AB de Villiers, not surprisingly, top the chart with 326 and 212 sixes, respectively. Kohli follows close behind with 190 IPL sixes.

Australian leg-spinner Adam Zampa, who has faced the wrath of Rohit's six-hitting abilities, compared him with Kohli and said in May 2020, 'The difference between Virat and Rohit is that Rohit is very much the six-hitter. Rohit likes to hit out of the park, he is one of those who can hit out of the park after three–four balls. Virat likes to play a little bit safer, along the ground. That is the difference between the two.'

Zampa has dismissed Rohit five times in international cricket, four times in ODIs and once in T20Is.

Nayar said that Rohit always had this tendency to hit sixes from his young days. 'He always had it to hit really big sixes. I remember at CCI (Brabourne Stadium), he hit the ball on to the roof. Sixes now have become smaller! He used to hit really big sixes. After his hamstring and shoulder injuries, his sixes have, though they are regular, become smaller. Because he had a tennis ball cricket background, he was known for hitting sixes. Short arm pull is very important in tennis ball cricket.'

Tennis ball cricket is a common sight in the maidans of Mumbai. One has to hit sixes frequently to remain in the fray. A regular stroke is the pull-shot, which Rohit has developed and mastered from his tennis ball cricket days. As a compulsive hooker of the cricket ball, Rohit is ready to hook or pull

anything short, more often clearing the boundary than falling to the fielders placed inside the rope.

Nayar recalled, 'When he wanted to hit big, he used to play that shot over mid-wicket or long-on. But his unique shot was over cover-point. It's not an easy shot for most people. He used to hit over sweeper cover and cover point. I saw him talk about it on Instagram recently. That was his unique shot. A lot of people hit sixes over mid-wicket. Not many hit sixes over cover-point. You need perfection to hit out of the ground. Once he gets going, he becomes very difficult to bowl to. He used to play all types of shots and all over the ground.'

TEN

Rohit and His Army of Fans

He has an imposing presence at the crease. Not a Chris Gayle-like personality that destroys the bowlers with an astonishing range of shots, but able to make an impact in his own way. Rohit Sharma, a batsman with a combination of silken drives and robust pulls, can be a subject worthy of a case study on how to convert your energy into a successful career.

That he emerged from the Bombay school of cricket is all the more baffling. Rohit is not the quintessential Bombay batsman—perfect in technique, builder of an innings brick by brick. The likes of Vijay Merchant, Vijay Manjrekar, Sunil Gavaskar, Dilip Vengsarkar, Sachin Tendulkar are more typical, known to promote correct batsmanship.

Rohit revives memories of a Sandeep Patil—playing on his terms and executing shots of variety, aggression being the driving force. Vengsarkar too was known for his attractive stroke play, but he curtailed his shots as his career progressed. Rohit is a brilliant run-getter at the crease, which sometimes leads him to play ambitious shots that cause his downfall and often lead to unjust criticism.

Vidyasagar Ayyappan, a Mumbai-based radio jockey who lives life cricket size, says Rohit is the batsman to watch. He says, 'You pitch it up to Rohit, he murders you. You pitch it short, he mutilates you. As a bowler your margin of error is wafer thin when you're up against Rohit. He smashed 276 sixes in international cricket since January 2016. No one else crossed even 160 sixes in the same period. A serial six hitter is an entertainer, by default... Rohit has many more aces up his sleeve than just being a six-hitting monster. He is without doubt, a modern-day great.'

Rohit stands tall on the huge canvas of entertaining batsmanship, his effortless stroke play leaving the bowlers crestfallen. His ability to convert even good deliveries into ordinary is impressive. He gave early indications of his awesome talent when noted Mumbai coach Dinesh Lad saw him first. 'He had so much time to play the ball,' remembered Lad. That quality actually clinched the place for Rohit.

For journalism student Charudutt Prabhu, a leg-spinner who follows the game passionately, Rohit represents the best image of a modern batsman who is proficient in all formats of the game.

'If there is a manual for being an impactful batsman, Rohit ticks all the boxes. His repertoire of strokes, innings construction and temperament make him one of the modern-day greats. A player of his calibre is what every team wishes to have.

'It was only six years after his debut for India his cricketing career started to blossom. Earlier, the talks on Rohit were how talented he was, but soon he, through his performances, emerged as a match-winner and a dependable batsman. Be it playing out the new ball or providing a solid start, the right-

hander has, over the years, been successful. He safeguards the Indian batting line-up in all three formats with ease. If Virender Sehwag brought dominance in opening batting, Rohit Sharma has brought assurance.'

True, Rohit has brought assurance. He has also created a legion of cricket fans who flock the venue to watch him. For Diya Valeja, a cricket fan, Rohit is the reason she came to love the game. Diya says, 'I was never a cricket fan before 2013. But being a true Mumbaikar, I used to watch bits and pieces from a few MI (Mumbai Indian) games because my father and grandfather would watch the IPL (Indian Premier League) like most Indian households. I remember watching a game of Mumbai Indians that season and the way Rohit played in that match, I was awestruck! For some reason it really made me want to watch more games and before I knew it, there I was, sitting on my sofa before every Mumbai Indians match waiting for the toss. Rohit Sharma is the reason why I have been following cricket since 2013–2014 and I have been in love with him, and the game, ever since.'

It can be demanding for a popular sportsman to keep the fans happy. But Rohit has a connect with them right from his early days with the Mumbai team. He appeals to the common cricket follower. Diya puts it aptly, 'The effortlessness with which he bats, hands down, is his most striking batting quality for me. Rohit makes cricket look so easy! He effortlessly hits the biggest of sixes and boundaries, especially his pull and cut shots, they're brilliant. I think I don't see a lot of people talking about his lifted shots over the V, he plays them so well! Most people call it his "lazy elegance" and I would agree. Once he gets

going, it's difficult to take your eyes off. He is an absolute treat to watch.'

Lazy elegance was best illustrated by England's David Gower, who won the hearts of his fans by dominating the bowlers with a caress here and a pat there and sending the ball racing all over the field. It was as if Gower did not want to hurt the bowler with a robust shot. Even his cut and pull shots were mostly a delicate execution of his awesome timing. For Ajinkya Pandharkar, a chartered accountant based in Mumbai, Rohit personifies the image of a cool mind at the crease.

'The best thing about Rohit's batting is the lazy elegance. He seems to have so much time to play the ball and time it to perfection. He is so hardworking. He has got loads of talent, sometimes mocked for having that, failed, again failed and finally he succeeded and then he never looked back till he became one of the best! I would love to ask him "What is the one thing which keeps you going and what will you tell yourself if you were a 12-year-old?" Also, "Advice you will give to a 12-year-old Rohit Sharma."'

The 12-year-old Rohit was obsessed with batting long at the nets and in matches. Nothing irked him more than losing his wicket to a loose shot. But then he always believed that his job as a batsman was to belt the ball. Sometimes the bowler would win the battle early, but not always.

Sachin Tendulkar, Virender Sehwag, Sourav Ganguly, V.V.S. Laxman, Yuvraj Singh, M.S. Dhoni, Virat Kohli have been some of the iconic batsmen who have commanded a huge fan-following with their sensational deeds in limited overs cricket. The modern generation of cricket fans loves the Rohit-like aggression on the field, batsman confronting

the bowler, the ensuing battle a treat for the connoisseurs of the game.

Behind the amazing stroke player that he is, Rohit has an enviable humility to his character. Diya, for whom this cricketer from Mumbai is a complete package of what a sports icon should be, says, 'I can confidently say that I have never seen a man as humble as Rohit. He will talk to you like he has known you for years. He remains grounded no matter what. And I think that is something we don't see a lot these days. His persistence, leadership skills, rags-to-riches story, and standing up for what he believes in with all the wonderful initiatives he takes up—whether it is rhino conservation or raising awareness about protecting the environment, I think all these things make him the perfect person to look up to.'

Here is an anecdote that brings out the role model in Rohit. Diya has been fortunate to meet him thrice and had this to share.

'I first met him back in 2016, as a nervous tenth grader who was about to give her preliminary exams. When I was introduced to him, I was shaking. He noticed that and immediately tried to lighten things up and made me feel extremely comfortable. The second time was just after MI's 2017 IPL victory and when we met him, coincidentally, the match highlights were going on in that room. He explained the last two overs ball by ball to us and what he was telling the bowlers to do. For a moment it felt like we were a part of the game. In April 2019, I was invited by MI with a few other fans to celebrate his birthday with him and we spent more than an hour together—he cut the cake with us, gave time and spoke to each one of us and even gave "us" presents. Imagine, someone of his stature spending time with his fans on his birthday. He is a gem. Meeting him

always feels like meeting a family member, he makes you feel that way.'

It is this aspect of Rohit that endears him to the cricket world. His smile is infectious and brings loads of pleasantness to the dressing room. He steps up to assume all the responsibility associated with a match-winner. Nothing perturbs him because of his self-belief. The greater the challenge, the better is Rohit's response.

That Rohit is a modest man is well established. He will be the first to acknowledge with a nod a good delivery by the opponent. Misdemeanours have not been a part of his behaviour, whether on or off the field. He loves to compete and seeks to take on the best. This makes him a strong cricketer, and his teammates have benefited from his positive attitude.

There is a firm belief in the Mumbai Indians and Team India dressing room that Rohit is the most calming influence during tough situations. He takes joy in motivating the partner in the middle, often taking on the best bowler of the day, and never shying from shielding his fellow batsman from challenges from the opponents. Throw Rohit a challenge and expect a robust response. Much to the delight of the spectators, this attacking opener often gives them a feast of runs.

Rohit grew up hearing tales of some legendary cricketers, some local heroes, and drew inspiration from the performances of players such as Wasim Jaffer and Amol Muzumdar, who served Mumbai cricket with distinction. The pride of representing Mumbai is not to be missed whenever Rohit turns out for his state. Rohit made a conscious effort not to copy anyone. He was always looking to establish his own identity and he did, emerging as an integral part of Indian team as well.

Rohit is a natural when it comes to taking charge at the crease. Just as a Viv Richards or a Sehwag, if the first ball presented to him a juicy opportunity to play a shot, Rohit does not hesitate. Sehwag's policy was that the ball was supposed to be hit. Just because a half-volley happens to be the first ball the batsman faces does not necessarily evoke a defensive shot. Rohit has always looked forward to establishing early dominance.

Manoj Prabhakar, a cricketer who worked hard on his batting, advocated a positive approach whatever be the challenge. He says, 'You don't gain by falling on defence just because the challenge is huge. I learnt early in my career never to discard my natural game. Sometimes it cost me my wicket. I am glad Rohit has not compromised with the task given to him. He is your best batsman after Kohli and must be given the freedom to pursue his natural flair. We have seen many times how Rohit walks in and takes charge in no time. That comes from his penchant to dominate.'

Rohit's approach to life was charted by his struggle to make it big. Travelling distances as a club cricketer, raised on the maidans of Mumbai to face a variety of opponents who would test his skills and temperament, Rohit learnt quickly that he had to be more consistent than the rest. He concentrated on getting big scores and was a dreaded batsman in Mumbai cricket as word spread of his talent of mocking the best of the bowlers.

To his credit, Rohit has never looked laboured at the crease. Poor form would leave his averages bleeding, but not once has he compromised his natural style for the sake of achieving a higher grade of averages. For a cricket follower like Ayyappan, Rohit is a phenomenal cricketer. A die-hard fan of the game, Ayyappan spends his free time analysing the careers of top cricketers. His

assessment of Rohit is as dramatic as the batsman's batting. Ayyappan says, 'Rohit is the ONLY opener who has opened in 200+ innings across international cricket and averages 50+. At a strike rate of 98.93, Rohit is second only to Adam Gilchrist (of Australia) who has a strike rate of 98.94 (0.01 more), among openers who have opened in 200+ international innings. At 61%, Rohit Sharma has the highest percentage of ODI wins among Indians.'

He digs up more interesting stats: 'In ODIs, Rohit Sharma has: 29 * 100+ scores; 16 * 125+ scores (2nd most); 8 * 150+ scores (most by anyone) and 3 * 200+ scores (most by anyone). These numbers show that Rohit is a modern-day great already, albeit in the limited overs format.'

Further analysis of Rohit's career by Ayyappan throws light on the batsman's versatility.

'He is a deadly combination of Damien Martyn's silken touch and Viv Richards' raw hitting power. He has something to offer in equal measure to a connoisseur and a millennial. The limited overs format needs people who can steal matches in quick time; Rohit has no match in his ability to take matches away from the opposition once he has his eyes in. But he is not perfect. Nobody is perfect. No batsman is perfect unless he masters the art of negotiating the moving Dukes ball, the moving Kookaburra, while batting higher up the order in his whites.'

For Rohit, the most glowing praise came from Sunil Gavaskar, the greatest opening batsman the game has seen. Gavaskar was the reason players like Tendulkar, Dravid, Sanjay Manjrekar took to the game. The maestro, an epitome

of perfection at the crease, described his admiration for Rohit when speaking to *India Today*.

'The way you see a Rohit Sharma opening the batting in one-day cricket, Test cricket smashing from the first over. That is what I wanted to play. Circumstances and, of course, lack of confidence in my ability did not allow me to do that. But when I see the next generation doing it, I am absolutely over the moon, I love watching the next generation because there you see progress. You see how they are setting the bar higher for the next generation.'

Rohit could not have asked for a bigger award for his batsmanship in all formats of the game.

This domineering batsmanship is what sets Rohit apart. Not one to make tall claims, he has always believed in making things happen by getting the bat to talk. Strange that some people could not digest his popularity and tried to create a wedge between him and Kohli at the end of the 2019 World Cup. Gavaskar was understandably furious. He had encountered similar issues when critics wrote about his fallout with Kapil Dev at the peak of their careers.

In his column in *Sportstar*, Gavaskar said Virat and Rohit may shout from the rooftops but the issue won't die.

'Every time Rohit fails there will be those who will nod their heads knowingly and wink, hinting he deliberately got out. Nobody even gives a thought to the fact that if a player fails he is likely to be dropped and so he would be hurting his own chances of survival in the squad. Whoever starts such stories is definitely not a well-wisher of Indian cricket. More often than not it's a frustrated player in the squad who gives wings to stories

like this. His envy and jealousy harm the team. Then, of course, it suits some administrators to play their own game of politics.'

Gavaskar also saw the role played by the media in encouraging such harsh stories that harmed Indian cricket. He wrote, 'For the media, it's manna from heaven and so while it can be suppressed when the cricket is on, the rest days between games is where the story gets fanned further. Kohli and Rohit are professionals and they will put their heads down and go out to win matches for India but the story won't stop even 20 years later.'

On his part, Kohli was candid. 'We've had no issues. If I don't like somebody, it shows on my face. I have also heard a lot in past few days, but if team atmosphere wasn't good, we couldn't have played well,' he said during a media interaction.

At another time, Kohli praised Rohit profusely for putting the T20 experience to good use in the 50-over format. In an interview with Cricinfo, Kohli said, 'I have never seen a guy, after he gets set, be so dangerous. He [Rohit] has scored double-hundreds in ODIs opening the innings. Could you have imagined all these things without gaining confidence from T20 cricket, where guys keep hitting so consistently that they build confidence to do it throughout 50 overs?'

It is hard to be a popular cricketer because the fans and the media put you under constant scrutiny. In Rohit's case, the intensity is great because the expectations are highest. The brand of cricket that he plays allows him to take the opponents by the scruff of the neck, and the audience loves it. Young cricketers on the circuit want to emulate his style and have to be cautioned by their coaches. Rohit is gifted. He has worked hard on his game. He has also built his personality to establish a warm connect

with his fans, the people he rates as the most important segment of cricket. There can't be a hero without fans.

What would a cricket fan ask of Rohit if given an opportunity for an interview? Diya, who was floored when Rohit recognized her when they met the second time, gushes, 'With all the adulation that surrounds cricket and cricketers, it is very easy to lose your humility, especially in a country like India where cricketers are worshipped. So I would want to ask him what keeps him so grounded even after being who he is today.'

It is not hard to find an answer. Rohit learnt a lesson early in his life from his coach Lad: 'Stay grounded when you achieve success.' Rohit has remembered those impactful words.

Notes

1. Cricinfo commentary from the match page
2. Over the phone on 12 May, 2020.
3. "'I Seriously Can't Believe It,' Rohit Sharma Recalls IPL Hat-Trick against Mumbai Indians." *Hindustan Times*, 9 May 2020. https://www.hindustantimes.com/cricket/i-seriously-can-t-believe-it-rohit-sharma-recalls-ipl-hat-trick-against-mumbai-indians/story-oAYiPoOCs0LDuyNNpCbvDO.html.
4. "Sharma's Been There, Done That." *Hindustan Times*, 7 May 2009. https://www.hindustantimes.com/cricket/sharma-s-been-there-done-that/story-4l8x3csxlxucE6wuwMH2jK.html.
5. Abraham, Derek. "IPL Auction: Rohit Sharma Comes Home to Mumbai." *DNA India*, 8 January 2011. https://www.dnaindia.com/sports/report-ipl-auction-rohit-sharma-comes-home-to-mumbai-1492148.
6. International, Asian News. "Not Being Picked for World Cup 2011 in India Saddest Moment of My Career: Rohit Sharma." *India Today*, 26 March 2020. https://www.indiatoday.in/sports/cricket/story/rohit-sharma-not-playing-in-world-cup-2011-saddest-moment-of-life-kevin-pietersen-1660018-2020-03-26.
7. cricinfo commentary from post-match presentation, match scoreboard page
8. Staff, ESPNcricinfo. "Champions League T20 Discontinued." ESPNcricinfo. *ESPNcricinfo*, 7 September 2017. https://www.

espncricinfo.com/story/_/id/20621995/champions-league-t20-discontinued.

9. Krishnan, G. "Will Open Batting This IPL Season: Rohit Sharma." *DNA India*, 20 March 2019. https://www.dnaindia.com/cricket/report-will-open-batting-this-ipl-season-rohit-sharma-2731157.

10. DH News Service. "Ponting to Lead Mumbai Indians in 2013 IPL." Deccan Herald. *DH News Service*, 21 February 2013. https://www.deccanherald.com/content/313797/ponting-lead-mumbai-indians-2013.html.

11. Instagram Live with R. Ashwin in mid-May 2020.

12. Cricinfo commentary match page.

13. "M33: KKR vs MI – Rohit Sharma Press Conference." Indian Premier League | IPLT20.com. Accessed 26 September 2020. https://www.iplt20.com/video/22798.

14. Singh, Priyam. "Rohit Sharma Names The Best Coach He Has Ever Played Under." CricketAddictor. *Cricketaddictor*, 4 April 2020. https://cricketaddictor.com/cricket/rohit-sharma-best-coach-ricky-ponting/.

15. Krishnan, G. "If You Find Meaning in Your Work, It Becomes a Passion: Nita Ambani." *DNA India*, 8 April 2015. https://www.dnaindia.com/sports/interview-if-you-find-meaning-in-your-work-it-becomes-a-passion-nita-ambani-2075571.

16. "Rohit Sharma's Captaincy in IPL Has Been Spot on: Ricky Ponting." News18. *News18*, 16 August 2015. https://www.news18.com/cricketnext/news/rohit-sharmas-captaincy-in-ipl-has-been-spot-on-ricky-ponting-979226.html.

17. "Rahul Chahar Thanks Rohit, Zaheer for IPL Success, Hopes Dream of Playing alongside Cousin Deepak Comes True." Cricket Country. *Cricket Country*, 29 July 2019. https://www.cricketcountry.com/news/rahul-chahar-thanks-rohit-sharma-zaheer-khan-for-ipl-success-hopes-dream-of-playing-alongside-cousin-deepak-chahar-comes-true-873348.

18. Nayar to me on 12 May 2020.

19. Nayak, Amarjeet. "Rohit Sharma Is Right: Ambati Rayudu Has Done Enough to Be India's Number 4 in World Cup 2019." Sports news. *Sportskeeda*, 5 November 2018. https://www.

sportskeeda.com/cricket/rohit-sharma-is-right-ambati-rayudu-has-done-enough-to-be-india-s-number-4-in-world-cup-2019.

20. "Rohit Sharma Has Learnt the Art of Captaincy from MS Dhoni: Ambati Rayudu." *CricTracker*, 4 May 2020. https://www.crictracker.com/rohit-sharma-has-learnt-the-art-of-captaincy-from-ms-dhoni-ambati-rayudu/.

21. "Lockdown Fun with Rohit Sharma." The Board of Control for Cricket in India, 6 May 2020. https://www.bcci.tv/videos/147262/lockdown-fun-with-rohit-sharma.

22. "Sachin Tendulkar 100th Century Celebration by Mukesh Ambani." YouTube. *Incredible India*, 16 November 2016. https://youtu.be/yVepuca0Qo0.

23. "'It Depends on...': Kevin Pietersen Says 'It's Difficult' for Virat Kohli to Break Sachin Tendulkar's 100 Centuries Record." *Hindustan Times*, 15 May 2020. https://www.hindustantimes.com/cricket/sachin-didn-t-have-same-aggression-on-field-pietersen-says-it-s-difficult-for-kohli-to-break-tendulkar-s-record/story-Fj12EjLPP7DbyCiWE7N8eP.html.

24. Cricinfo commentary match page.

25. Sahi, Lokendra Pratap. "Kumar Sangakkara's Praise: Great Job, Well Done." ICC Cricket World Cup 2019: Great job and well done, says Kumar Sangakkara – Telegraph India. *Telegraph India*, 6 July 2019. https://www.telegraphindia.com/sport/cricket/icc-cricket-world-cup-2019-great-job-and-well-done-says-kumar-sangakkara/cid/1693982.

26. "Will Take Positives from These Knocks: Rohit." The Board of Control for Cricket in India, 20 October 2019. https://www.bcci.tv/videos/135216/will-take-positives-from-these-knocks-rohit.

27. "Proud of the Collective Team Effort: Virat Kohli." The Board of Control for Cricket in India, 22 October 2019. https://www.bcci.tv/videos/135607/proud-of-the-collective-team-effort-virat-kohli.

28. "Lockdown Fun with Rohit Sharma." The Board of Control for Cricket in India, 6 May 2020. https://www.bcci.tv/videos/147262/lockdown-fun-with-rohit-sharma.

Rohit Sharma in Facts and Figures

– RAJNEESH GUPTA

- **Full name:** Rohit Gurunath Sharma
- **Born:** 30 April 1987, Bansod, Nagpur (Maharashtra)
- **Style:** Right-handed batsman & right-arm offbreak bowler
- **Teams:** Mumbai Under-17s, India Under-17s, West Zone Under-17s, National Cricket Academy, Mumbai Under-19s, West Zone Under-19s, India Under-19s, Mumbai Cricket Association President's XI, West Zone, India A, Indian Oil Corporation, India Red, Mumbai Under-22s, Mumbai, Indians, India, Deccan Chargers, Mumbai Cricket Association XI, Indian Board President's XI, India Green, Mumbai Indians, India Blue.
- **First-class debut:** India A vs New Zealand A at Darwin, 11 July 2006 (made 57 & 22)
- **Highest first-class score:** 309* (458 mins, 322 balls, 38 fours, 4 sixes), Mumbai vs Gujarat at Mumbai BS in December 2009
- **Best first-class bowling (innings):** 4-41 for India A vs West Indies A at Bridgetown in June 2012
- **Best first-class bowling (match):** 5-85 for India A vs West Indies A at Bridgetown in June 2012
- **Test debut:** vs West Indies at Kolkata in November 2013
- **Highest Test score:** 212 (403 mins, 255 balls, 28 fours, 6 sixes) vs South Africa at Ranchi in October 2019
- **Best Test bowling (innings):** 1-26 vs England at Southampton in July 2014
- **Best Test bowling (match):** 1-35 vs Australia at Adelaide in December 2014

FIRST-CLASS CAREER
Batting and Fielding

	Mts	Inns	NO	Runs	Hs	Avg	SR	100	50	0	4s	6s	Ct
Tests	32	53	7	2141	212	46.54	59.25	6	10	4	216	52	31
Ranji Trophy	42	60	6	3892	309*	72.07	68.83	14	15	3	475	51	31
Duleep Trophy	4	8	1	310	116	44.28	63.52	1	1	0	35	7	4
Irani Trophy	3	5	0	49	21	9.80	48.03	0	0	1	5	1	3
'A' Tests	6	10	0	384	119	38.40	47.76	1	2	0	39	9	4
Other First-class	5	7	2	342	105	68.40	61.29	1	2	0	48	1	2
TOTAL	92	143	16	7118	309*	56.04	63.44	23	30	8	818	121	75

Bowling

	Mts	Balls	Runs	Wkts	Best	Avg	RPO	5WI	10WM
Tests	32	370	216	2	1-26	108.00	3.50	0	0
Ranji Trophy	42	870	447	5	1-1	89.40	3.08	0	0
Duleep Trophy	4	18	12	0	–	–	4.00	0	0
Irani Trophy	3	192	137	5	3-23	27.40	4.28	0	0
'A' Tests	6	594	286	11	4-41	26.00	2.88	0	0
Other First-class	5	96	48	1	1-12	48.00	3.00	0	0
TOTAL	92	2140	1146	24	4-41	47.75	3.21	0	0

- **List 'A' debut:** For West Zone vs Central Zone at Gwalior, 25 February 2006 (Deodhar Trophy) (made 31* off 47 balls)
- **Highest List 'A' score:** 264 (173 balls, 33 fours, 9 sixes) for India vs Sri Lanka at Kolkata, 13 November 2014 (One-day international)

- **Best List 'A' bowling:** 4-28 for Mumbai vs Saurashtra at Vadodara, 13 February 2011 (Vijay Hazare Trophy)
- **ODI debut:** vs Ireland at Belfast, 23 June 2007 (did not bat)
- **Highest ODI score:** 264 (173 balls, 33 fours, 9 sixes) vs Sri Lanka at Kolkata, 13 November 2014
- **Best ODI bowling:** 2-27 vs West Indies at Kingston, 28 June 2009
- **ODI captaincy record:** Played 10, Won 8, Lost 2, Win% – 80.00

LIST 'A' CAREER

Batting and Fielding

	Mts	Inns	NO	Runs	Hs	Avg	SR	100	50	0	4s	6s	Ct
One-Day Internationals	224	217	32	9115	264	49.27	88.92	29	43	13	817	244	77
Vijay Hazare Trophy	25	24	2	823	100	37.40	92.05	1	5	3	78	19	10
Deodhar Trophy	14	14	3	402	142*	36.54	75.28	1	1	0	38	7	4
Challenger Series	11	10	1	323	117*	35.88	83.24	1	0	1	35	4	5
'A' One-Day Internationals	14	14	1	477	66	36.69		0	4	0	39+	8+	2
EurAsia Cricket Series	4	3	0	132	62	44.00	90.41	0	2	0	9	2	2
Other Limited Overs	3	2	1	85	61*	85.00	79.43	0	1	0	9	1	1
TOTAL	295	284	40	11357	264	46.54		32	56	17	1025+	285+	101

Bowling

Type	Mts	Balls	Runs	Wkts	Best	Avg	RPO	4W
One-Day Internationals	224	593	515	8	2-27	64.37	5.21	0
Vijay Hazare Trophy	25	468	378	13	4-28	29.07	4.84	1
Deodhar Trophy	14	72	48	4	2-27	12.00	4.00	0
Challenger Series	11	108	105	2	1-4	52.50	5.83	0
'A' One-day Internationals	14	84	67	3	2-32	22.33	4.78	0
EurAsia Cricket Series	4	12	12	0	–		6.00	0
Other Limited Overs	3	30	37	0	–		7.40	0
TOTAL	295	1367	1162	30	4-28	38.73	5.10	1

- **Twenty20 debut:** For Mumbai vs Baroda at Mumbai WS, 3 April 2007 (Vijay Hazare Trophy) (made 40* off 37 balls and took 3-15 in 3 overs)
- **Highest Twenty20 score:** 118 for India vs Sri Lanka at Indore, 22 December 2017 (Twenty20 International)
- **Best Twenty20 bowling:** 2-25 for Royal Challengers Bengaluru vs Deccan Chargers at Hyderabad, 25 May 2008 (IPL)
- **T20I debut:** vs England at Durban, 19 September 2007 (Did not bat and bowl)
- **Highest T20I score:** 118 (43 balls, 12 fours, 10 sixes) vs Sri Lanka at Indore, 22 December 2017
- **Best T20I bowling:** 1-22 vs Sri Lanka at Nagpur, 9 December 2009
- **T20I captaincy record:** Played 19, Won 15, Lost 4, Win% – 78.95

TWENTY20 CAREER

Batting and Fielding

	Mts	Inns	NO	Runs	Hs	Avg	SR	100	50	0	4s	6s	Ct
Twenty20 Internationals	108	100	15	2773	118	32.62	138.78	4	21	6	245	127	40
Indian Premier League	188	183	28	4898	109*	31.60	130.82	1	36	12	431	194	83
Syed Mushtaq Ali Trophy	17	17	3	535	101*	38.21	141.53	1	1	1	56	19	6
Champions League	11	11	1	322	51	32.20	126.77	0	1	0	24	16	2
'A' Twenty20 Internationals	2	2	0	55	52	27.50	137.50	0	1	0	5	2	0
Other Twenty20	2	2	0	59	30	29.50	120.40	0	0	0	2	3	0
TOTAL	328	315	47	8642	118	32.24	133.71	6	60	19	763	361	131

Bowling

	Mts	Balls	Runs	Wkts	Best	Avg	RPO	3W
Twenty20 Internationals	108	68	113	1	1-22	113.00	9.97	0
Indian Premier League	188	332	440	15	4-6	29.33	7.95	2
Syed Mushtaq Ali Trophy	17	198	227	11	3-15	20.63	6.87	1
Champions League	11	12	13	0	–		6.50	0
'A' Twenty20 Internationals	2	12	17	2	2-4	8.50	8.50	0
Other Twenty20	2	6	7	0	–		7.00	0
TOTAL	328	628	817	29	4-6	28.17	7.80	1

ROHIT SHARMA IN TEST CRICKET
Performance in Each Match

Start Date	Against	Venue	Batting	Bowling	Fielding
06-11-2013	West Indies	Kolkata	177		1 ct
14-11-2013	West Indies	Mumbai WS	111*		2 cts
18-12-2013	South Africa	Johannesburg	14 & 6		1 ct
26-12-2013	South Africa	Durban	0 & 25	0-29 & 0-10	
06-02-2014	New Zealand	Auckland	72 & 19	0-12 & 0-3	2 cts
14-02-2014	New Zealand	Wellington	0 & 31*	dnb & 0-40	2 cts
27-07-2014	England	Southampton	28 & 6	1-26 & 0-32	
09-12-2014	Australia	Adelaide	43 & 6	dnb & 1-35	1 ct
17-12-2014	Australia	Brisbane	32 & 0	0-10	1 ct
06-01-2015	Australia	Sydney	53 & 39		
10-06-2015	Bangladesh	Fatullah	6		3 cts
12-08-2015	Sri Lanka	Galle	9 & 4		2 cts
20-08-2015	Sri Lanka	Colombo PSS	79 & 34		
28-08-2015	Sri Lanka	Colombo SSC	26 & 50		1 ct
25-11-2015	South Africa	Nagpur	2 & 23		1 ct
03-12-2015	South Africa	Delhi	1 & 0		
09-08-2016	West Indies	Gros Islet	9 & 41		2 cts
18-08-2016	West Indies	Port-of-Spain			1 ct
22-09-2016	New Zealand	Kanpur	35 & 68*	0-5	2 cts
30-09-2016	New Zealand	Kolkata	2 & 82		
08-10-2016	New Zealand	Indore	51*		
24-11-2017	Sri Lanka	Nagpur	102*		1 ct
02-12-2017	Sri Lanka	Delhi	65 & 50*		
05-01-2018	South Africa	Cape Town	11 & 10		1 ct
13-01-2018	South Africa	Centurion	10 & 47		
06-12-2018	Australia	Adelaide	37 & 1		1 ct
26-12-2018	Australia	Melbourne	63* & 5		
02-10-2019	South Africa	Visakhapatnam	176 & 127	0-7 & 0-3	
10-10-2019	South Africa	Pune	14	0-0 & 0-4	3 cts
19-10-2019	South Africa	Ranchi	212		1 ct
14-11-2019	Bangladesh	Indore	6		1 ct
22-11-2019	Bangladesh	Kolkata	21		1 ct

dnb = did not bowl

Innings Break-up

Runs	Innings
0	4
1-9	13
10-29	11
30-49	9
50-89	10
90-99	0
100-149	3
150-199	2
200+	1

Mode of Dismissals

	Innings
Caught in the field	18
Caught by keeper	9
Bowled	9
Leg before wicket	8
Stumped	2
Run out	0
Hit wicket	0
Completed innings	46
(not out)	7

Performance Against Each Country

	Mts	Inns	NO	Runs	Hs	Avg	SR	100	50	0	4s	6s
vs Australia	5	10	1	279	63*	31.00	47.61	0	2	1	23	8
vs Bangladesh	3	3	0	33	21	11.00	56.89	0	0	0	4	1
vs England	1	2	0	34	28	17.00	38.20	0	0	0	3	0
vs New Zealand	5	9	3	360	82	60.00	55.72	0	4	1	37	6
vs South Africa	9	16	0	678	212	42.37	64.63	3	0	2	76	22
vs Sri Lanka	5	9	2	419	102*	59.85	62.07	1	4	0	36	8
vs West Indies	4	4	1	338	177	112.66	66.27	2	0	0	37	7
TOTAL	32	53	7	2141	212	46.54	59.25	6	10	4	216	52

Performance in Each Country

	Mts	Inns	NO	Runs	Hs	Avg	SR	100	50	0	4s	6s
in Australia	5	10	1	279	63*	31.00	47.61	0	2	1	23	8
in Bangladesh	1	1	0	6	6	6.00	66.66	0	0	0	1	0
in England	1	2	0	34	28	17.00	38.20	0	0	0	3	0
in India	14	20	5	1325	212	88.33	69.29	6	5	1	143	33
in New Zealand	2	4	1	122	72	40.66	43.72	0	1	1	14	1
in South Africa	4	8	0	123	47	15.37	42.12	0	0	1	13	2
in Sri Lanka	3	6	0	202	79	33.66	55.49	0	2	0	16	5
in West Indies	2	2	0	50	41	25.00	60.97	0	0	0	3	3

	Mts	Inns	NO	Runs	Hs	Avg	SR	100	50	0	4s	6s
Home	14	20	5	1325	212	88.33	69.29	6	5	1	143	33
Away	18	33	2	816	79	26.32	47.97	0	5	3	73	19

Performance in Each Calendar Year

	Mts	Inns	NO	Runs	Hs	Avg	SR	100	50	0	4s	6s
2013	4	6	1	333	177	66.60	62.83	2	0	1	38	5
2014	5	10	1	237	72	26.33	44.54	0	1	2	26	2
2015	7	13	0	326	79	25.07	48.65	0	3	1	25	10
2016	5	7	2	288	82	57.60	64.14	0	3	0	26	8
2017	2	3	2	217	102*	217.00	69.77	1	2	0	20	3
2018	4	8	1	184	63*	26.28	47.30	0	1	0	16	4
2019	5	6	0	556	212	92.66	75.95	3	0	0	65	20

Performance at Each Position

	Mts	Inns	NO	Runs	Hs	Avg	SR	100	50	0	4s	6s
2nd position	5	6	0	556	212	92.66	75.95	3	0	0	65	20
3rd position	4	5	0	107	53	21.40	41.63	0	1	1	9	4
4th position	1	1	0	4	4	4.00	25.00	0	0	0	1	0
5th position	9	16	1	437	79	29.13	48.55	0	3	1	38	10
6th position	16	25	6	1037	177	54.57	60.71	3	6	2	103	18

Performance in Each Match Innings

	Mts	Inns	NO	Runs	Hs	Avg	SR	100	50	0	4s	6s
1st match innings	18	18	2	824	212	51.50	62.70	2	4	1	87	25
2nd match innings	13	13	2	643	177	58.45	55.76	3	2	1	70	9
3rd match innings	15	14	2	512	127	42.66	69.75	1	4	2	43	15
4th match innings	8	8	1	162	47	23.14	39.32	0	0	0	16	3

	Mts	Inns	NO	Runs	Hs	Avg	SR	100	50	0	4s	6s
1st team innings	31	31	4	1467	212	54.33	59.46	5	6	2	157	34
2nd team innings	23	22	3	674	127	35.47	58.81	1	4	2	59	18

Performance in Day and Day/Night Matches

	Mts	Inns	NO	Runs	Hs	Avg	SR	100	50	0	4s	6s
Day match	31	52	7	2120	212	47.11	59.25	6	10	4	214	51
Day/night match	1	1	0	21	21	21.00	60.00	0	0	0	2	1

Performance in Won/Lost/Drawn Matches

	Mts	Inns	NO	Runs	Hs	Avg	SR	100	50	0	4s	6s
in WON matches	18	28	5	1555	212	67.60	65.72	6	6	1	155	42
in LOST matches	8	16	0	322	72	20.12	45.41	0	1	2	35	4
in DRAWN matches	6	9	2	264	65	37.71	49.07	0	3	1	26	6

ROHIT SHARMA IN ONE-DAY INTERNATIONALS

Performance in Each Match

Date	Against	Venue	Batting	Bowling	Fielding
23-06-2007	Ireland	Belfast			1 ct
26-06-2007	South Africa	Belfast	8 (9)	0-3 (1)	1 ct
05-10-2007	Australia	Hyderabad	1 (4)		
18-11-2007	Pakistan	Jaipur	52 (61)		1 ct

Date	Against	Venue	Batting	Bowling	Fielding
03-02-2008	Australia	Brisbane	29 (43)		
05-02-2008	Sri Lanka	Brisbane	0 (2)		
10-02-2008	Australia	Melbourne	39* (61)		1 ct
12-02-2008	Sri Lanka	Canberra	70* (64)		
17-02-2008	Australia	Adelaide	1 (3)		1 ct
19-02-2008	Sri Lanka	Adelaide	24 (36)		
24-02-2008	Australia	Sydney	1 (3)		1 ct
26-02-2008	Sri Lanka	Hobart	3* (7)		1 ct
02-03-2008	Australia	Sydney	66 (87)	0-5 (1)	1 ct
04-03-2008	Australia	Brisbane	2 (5)		
10-06-2008	Pakistan	Mirpur	9 (27)		1 ct
12-06-2008	Bangladesh	Mirpur	26 (43)		
14-06-2008	Pakistan	Mirpur	24 (27)		1 ct
25-06-2008	Hong Kong	Karachi	11 (29)		
26-06-2008	Pakistan	Karachi	0* (1)		
28-06-2008	Bangladesh	Karachi	22 (23)		
02-07-2008	Pakistan	Karachi	58 (71)		
03-07-2008	Sri Lanka	Karachi	22* (28)	0-4 (1)	
06-07-2008	Sri Lanka	Karachi	3 (8)	0-11 (3)	1 ct
18-08-2008	Sri Lanka	Dambulla	19 (31)	0-11 (2.5)	
20-08-2008	Sri Lanka	Dambulla	0 (2)		
24-08-2008	Sri Lanka	Colombo RPS	32 (32)	0-9 (1)	
27-08-2008	Sri Lanka	Colombo RPS	18 (23)	0-13 (4)	
29-08-2008	Sri Lanka	Colombo RPS	3 (5)	0-7 (2)	
14-11-2008	England	Rajkot	11* (8)		
17-11-2008	England	Indore	3 (13)		
20-11-2008	England	Kanpur	28 (41)		
26-11-2008	England	Cuttack	8* (10)		
28-01-2009	Sri Lanka	Dambulla	25* (30)	0-22 (4)	1 ct
05-02-2009	Sri Lanka	Colombo RPS	4* (6)		2 cts

Date	Against	Venue	Batting	Bowling	Fielding
08-02-2009	Sri Lanka	Colombo RPS	15 (22)	0-13 (2)	1 ct
11-03-2009	New Zealand	Hamilton			1 ct
14-03-2009	New Zealand	Auckland	43* (74)		
26-06-2009	West Indies	Kingston	4 (12)		2 cts
28-06-2009	West Indies	Kingston	0 (2)	2-27 (8)	
03-07-2009	West Indies	Gros Islet	11 (9)	0-7 (1)	
05-07-2009	West Indies	Gros Islet			
27-02-2010	South Africa	Ahmedabad	48 (61)	0-28 (3)	
28-05-2010	Zimbabwe	Bulawayo	114 (119)	0-5 (1)	
30-05-2010	Sri Lanka	Bulawayo	101* (100)		
03-06-2010	Zimbabwe	Harare	13 (25)		
05-06-2010	Sri Lanka	Harare	32 (40)		
16-06-2010	Bangladesh	Dambulla	0 (1)	1-5 (1)	
19-06-2010	Pakistan	Dambulla	22 (24)		
22-06-2010	Sri Lanka	Dambulla	69 (73)	0-9 (1)	
24-06-2010	Sri Lanka	Dambulla	41 (52)		
10-08-2010	New Zealand	Dambulla	4 (11)		
16-08-2010	Sri Lanka	Dambulla	0 (2)		1 ct
22-08-2010	Sri Lanka	Dambulla	11 (21)		
28-08-2010	Sri Lanka	Dambulla	5 (9)		2 cts
07-12-2010	New Zealand	Bangalore	44 (48)	0-19 (4)	1 ct
10-12-2010	New Zealand	Chennai			1 ct
12-01-2011	South Africa	Durban	11 (27)	2-30 (7)	1 ct
15-01-2011	South Africa	Johannesburg	9 (14)	1-12 (2)	
18-01-2011	South Africa	Cape Town	23 (45)	0-5 (1)	
21-01-2011	South Africa	Port Elizabeth	1 (6)	0-6 (2)	
23-01-2011	South Africa	Centurion	5 (8)	0-14 (2)	
06-06-2011	West Indies	Port-of-Spain	68* (75)		1 ct
08-06-2011	West Indies	Port-of-Spain	7* (14)		
11-06-2011	West Indies	North Sound	86* (91)		

Date	Against	Venue	Batting	Bowling	Fielding
13-06-2011	West Indies	North Sound	39 (47)		
16-06-2011	West Indies	Kingston	57 (72)		
03-09-2011	England	Chester-le-Street	0* (1)		
29-11-2011	West Indies	Cuttack	72 (99)	0-8 (2)	
02-12-2011	West Indies	Visakhapatnam	90* (98)		
05-12-2011	West Indies	Ahmedabad	95 (100)		
08-12-2011	West Indies	Indore	27 (16)	0-39 (5)	1 ct
11-12-2011	West Indies	Chennai	21 (26)		
05-02-2012	Australia	Melbourne	21 (21)	1-17 (2)	
08-02-2012	Sri Lanka	Perth	10 (17)		2 cts
12-02-2012	Australia	Adelaide	33 (41)	0-15 (2)	
14-02-2012	Sri Lanka	Adelaide	15 (27)	0-10 (2)	
19-02-2012	Australia	Brisbane	0 (5)	1-17 (3)	1 ct
13-03-2012	Sri Lanka	Mirpur		0-14 (3)	
16-03-2012	Bangladesh	Mirpur	4 (6)	0-13 (2)	2 cts
18-03-2012	Pakistan	Mirpur	68 (83)	0-19 (3)	
21-07-2012	Sri Lanka	Hambantota	5 (8)		
24-07-2012	Sri Lanka	Hambantota	0 (5)		
28-07-2012	Sri Lanka	Colombo RPS	0 (1)	0-4 (1)	
31-07-2012	Sri Lanka	Colombo RPS	4 (14)	0-6 (2)	
04-08-2012	Sri Lanka	Pallekele	4 (9)	0-23 (6)	
30-12-2012	Pakistan	Chennai	4 (14)		1 ct
23-01-2013	England	Mohali	83 (93)		
27-01-2013	England	Dharamsala	4 (9)		
06-06-2013	South Africa	Cardiff	65 (81)		
11-06-2013	West Indies	The Oval	52 (56)		
15-06-2013	Pakistan	Birmingham	18 (32)		1 ct
20-06-2013	Sri Lanka	Cardiff	33 (50)		
23-06-2013	England	Birmingham	9 (14)		
30-06-2013	West Indies	Kingston	60 (89)		

Date	Against	Venue	Batting	Bowling	Fielding
02-07-2013	Sri Lanka	Kingston	5 (13)		
05-07-2013	West Indies	Port-of-Spain	46 (78)		
09-07-2013	Sri Lanka	Port-of-Spain	48* (83)		
11-07-2013	Sri Lanka	Port-of-Spain	58 (89)		
24-07-2013	Zimbabwe	Harare	20 (40)		
26-07-2013	Zimbabwe	Harare	1 (7)		
28-07-2013	Zimbabwe	Harare	14 (21)		
01-08-2013	Zimbabwe	Bulawayo	64* (90)		1 ct
13-10-2013	Australia	Pune	42 (47)		1 ct
16-10-2013	Australia	Jaipur	141* (123)		
19-10-2013	Australia	Mohali	11 (22)		
23-10-2013	Australia	Ranchi	9* (13)		1 ct
30-10-2013	Australia	Nagpur	79 (89)		
02-11-2013	Australia	Bangalore	209 (158)		
21-11-2013	West Indies	Kochi	72 (81)	0-4 (2)	
24-11-2013	West Indies	Visakhapatnam	12 (19)		
27-11-2013	West Indies	Kanpur	4 (14)		
05-12-2013	South Africa	Johannesburg	18 (43)		
08-12-2013	South Africa	Durban	19 (26)		1 ct
11-12-2013	South Africa	Centurion			1 ct
19-01-2014	New Zealand	Napier	3 (23)		
22-01-2014	New Zealand	Hamilton	20 (34)		
25-01-2014	New Zealand	Auckland	39 (38)		
28-01-2014	New Zealand	Hamilton	79 (94)		
31-01-2014	New Zealand	Wellington	4 (13)		1 ct
26-02-2014	Bangladesh	Fatullah	21 (29)		1 ct
28-02-2014	Sri Lanka	Fatullah	13 (28)	0-29 (5)	2 cts
02-03-2014	Pakistan	Mirpur	56 (58)		
05-03-2014	Afghanistan	Mirpur	18* (24)		
27-08-2014	England	Cardiff	52 (87)		

Date	Against	Venue	Batting	Bowling	Fielding
13-11-2014	Sri Lanka	Kolkata	264 (173)		
16-11-2014	Sri Lanka	Ranchi	9 (12)		1 ct
18-01-2015	Australia	Melbourne	138 (139)		
15-02-2015	Pakistan	Adelaide	15 (20)		
22-02-2015	South Africa	Melbourne	0 (6)		
28-02-2015	United Arab Emirates	Perth	57* (55)		
06-03-2015	West Indies	Perth	7 (18)		
10-03-2015	Ireland	Hamilton	64 (66)	0-21 (3)	
14-03-2015	Zimbabwe	Auckland	16 (21)		1 ct
19-03-2015	Bangladesh	Melbourne	137 (126)		
26-03-2015	Australia	Sydney	34 (48)		2 cts
18-06-2015	Bangladesh	Mirpur	63 (68)		3 cts
21-06-2015	Bangladesh	Mirpur	0 (2)		
24-06-2015	Bangladesh	Mirpur	29 (29)		
11-10-2015	South Africa	Kanpur	150 (133)		
14-10-2015	South Africa	Indore	3 (10)		
18-10-2015	South Africa	Rajkot	65 (74)		
22-10-2015	South Africa	Chennai	21 (19)		
25-10-2015	South Africa	Mumbai WS	16 (20)		
12-01-2016	Australia	Perth	171* (163)	0-11 (1)	
15-01-2016	Australia	Brisbane	124 (127)		
17-01-2016	Australia	Melbourne	6 (11)		
20-01-2016	Australia	Canberra	41 (25)		1 ct
23-01-2016	Australia	Sydney	99 (108)		1 ct
16-10-2016	New Zealand	Dharamsala	14 (26)		1 ct
20-10-2016	New Zealand	Delhi	15 (27)		1 ct
23-10-2016	New Zealand	Mohali	13 (21)		
26-10-2016	New Zealand	Ranchi	11 (19)		1 ct
29-10-2016	New Zealand	Visakhapatnam	70 (65)		
04-06-2017	Pakistan	Birmingham	91 (119)		

Date	Against	Venue	Batting	Bowling	Fielding
08-06-2017	Sri Lanka	The Oval	78 (79)		
11-06-2017	South Africa	The Oval	12 (20)		
15-06-2017	Bangladesh	Birmingham	123* (129)		
18-06-2017	Pakistan	The Oval	0 (3)		
20-08-2017	Sri Lanka	Dambulla	4 (13)		
24-08-2017	Sri Lanka	Pallekele	54 (45)		1 ct
27-08-2017	Sri Lanka	Pallekele	124* (145)		1 ct
31-08-2017	Sri Lanka	Colombo RPS	104 (88)		
03-09-2017	Sri Lanka	Colombo RPS	16 (20)		
17-09-2017	Australia	Chennai	28 (44)		
21-09-2017	Australia	Kolkata	7 (14)		
24-09-2017	Australia	Indore	71 (62)		
28-09-2017	Australia	Bangalore	65 (55)		
01-10-2017	Australia	Nagpur	125 (109)		
22-10-2017	New Zealand	Mumbai WS	20 (18)		
25-10-2017	New Zealand	Pune	7 (19)		
29-10-2017	New Zealand	Kanpur	147 (138)		
10-12-2017	Sri Lanka	Dharamsala	2 (13)		
13-12-2017	Sri Lanka	Mohali	208* (153)		1 ct
17-12-2017	Sri Lanka	Visakhapatnam	7 (14)		1 ct
01-02-2018	South Africa	Durban	20 (30)		
04-02-2018	South Africa	Centurion	15 (17)		
07-02-2018	South Africa	Cape Town	0 (6)		
10-02-2018	South Africa	Johannesburg	5 (13)		1 ct
13-02-2018	South Africa	Port Elizabeth	115 (126)		1 ct
16-02-2018	South Africa	Centurion	15 (13)		
12-07-2018	England	Nottingham	137* (114)		
14-07-2018	England	Lord's	15 (26)		1 ct
17-07-2018	England	Leeds	2 (18)		
18-09-2018	Hong Kong	Dubai	23 (22)		1 ct
19-09-2018	Pakistan	Dubai	52 (39)		

Date	Against	Venue	Batting	Bowling	Fielding
21-09-2018	Bangladesh	Dubai	83* (104)		
23-09-2018	Pakistan	Dubai	111* (119)		1 ct
28-09-2018	Bangladesh	Dubai	48 (55)		
21-10-2018	West Indies	Guwahati	152* (117)		
24-10-2018	West Indies	Visakhapatnam	4 (8)		1 ct
27-10-2018	West Indies	Pune	8 (9)		2 cts
29-10-2018	West Indies	Mumbai BS	162 (137)		3 cts
01-11-2018	West Indies	Karyavattom	63* (56)		
12-01-2019	Australia	Sydney	133 (129)		1 ct
15-01-2019	Australia	Adelaide	43 (52)		
18-01-2019	Australia	Melbourne	9 (17)		1 ct
23-01-2019	New Zealand	Napier	11 (24)		1 ct
26-01-2019	New Zealand	Mount Maunganui	87 (96)		
28-01-2019	New Zealand	Mount Maunganui	62 (77)		1 ct
31-01-2019	New Zealand	Hamilton	7 (23)		
03-02-2019	New Zealand	Wellington	2 (16)		
02-03-2019	Australia	Hyderabad	37 (66)		
05-03-2019	Australia	Nagpur	0 (6)		
08-03-2019	Australia	Ranchi	14 (14)		
10-03-2019	Australia	Mohali	95 (92)		
13-03-2019	Australia	Delhi	56 (89)		
05-06-2019	South Africa	Southampton	122* (144)		1 ct
09-06-2019	Australia	The Oval	57 (70)		
16-06-2019	Pakistan	Manchester	140 (113)		
22-06-2019	Afghanistan	Southampton	1 (10)		
27-06-2019	West Indies	Manchester	18 (23)		1 ct
30-06-2019	England	Birmingham	102 (109)		1 ct
02-07-2019	Bangladesh	Birmingham	104 (92)		
06-07-2019	Sri Lanka	Leeds	103 (94)		1 ct

Date	Against	Venue	Batting	Bowling	Fielding
09-07-2019	New Zealand	Manchester	1 (4)		
08-08-2019	West Indies	Providence			
11-08-2019	West Indies	Port-of-Spain	18 (34)		
14-08-2019	West Indies	Port-of-Spain	10 (6)		
15-12-2019	West Indies	Chennai	36 (56)		
18-12-2019	West Indies	Visakhapatnam	159 (138)		
22-12-2019	West Indies	Cuttack	63 (63)		
14-01-2020	Australia	Mumbai WS	10 (15)		
17-01-2020	Australia	Rajkot	42 (44)		
19-01-2020	Australia	Bangalore	119 (128)		

Innings Break-Up

Runs	Innings
0	15
1–9	50
10–29	59
30–49	21
50–89	38
90–99	5
100–149	21
150–199	5
200+	3

Mode of Dismissals

	Innings
caught in the field	86
caught by keeper	36
bowled	29
leg before wicket	18
run out	13
stumped	3
hit wicket	0
Completed innings	185
(not out)	32

Performance Against Each Country

	Mts	Inns	NO	Runs	Hs	Avg	SR	100	50	0	4s	6s
vs Afghanistan	2	2	1	19	18*	19.00	55.88	0	0	0	1	0
vs Australia	40	40	4	2208	209	61.33	93.87	8	8	2	178	76
vs Bangladesh	13	13	2	660	137	60.00	93.35	3	2	2	54	19
vs England	13	13	4	454	137*	50.44	83.60	2	2	0	54	6
vs Hong Kong	2	2	0	34	23	17.00	66.66	0	0	0	4	0
vs Ireland	2	1	0	64	64	64.00	96.96	0	1	0	3	3
vs New Zealand	24	22	1	703	147	33.47	77.42	1	4	0	57	25
vs Pakistan	16	16	2	720	140	51.42	88.77	2	6	1	64	16
vs South Africa	25	24	1	766	150	33.30	80.54	3	2	2	80	18
vs Sri Lanka	46	45	9	1665	264	46.25	93.22	6	5	5	153	41
vs U.A.E.	1	1	1	57	57*	–	103.63	0	1	0	10	1
vs West Indies	33	31	6	1523	162	60.92	91.58	3	11	1	142	34
vs Zimbabwe	7	7	1	242	114	40.33	74.92	1	1	0	17	5
TOTAL	224	217	32	9115	264	49.27	88.92	29	43	13	817	244

Performance in Each Country

	Mts	Inns	NO	Runs	Hs	Avg	SR	100	50	0	4s	6s
in Australia	30	30	5	1328	171*	53.12	90.58	5	4	3	111	34
in Bangladesh	13	12	1	331	68	30.09	78.06	0	3	1	27	7
in England	24	24	4	1335	140	66.75	89.71	7	6	1	139	27
in India	65	64	8	3528	264	63.00	99.57	11	15	1	342	115
in Ireland	2	1	0	8	8	8.00	88.88	0	0	0	0	0
in New Zealand	14	13	1	437	87	36.41	72.95	0	4	0	28	18
in Pakistan	6	6	2	116	58	29.00	72.50	0	1	0	8	0
in South Africa	14	13	0	256	115	19.69	68.44	1	0	1	28	6
in Sri Lanka	26	26	3	583	124*	25.34	84.24	2	2	5	56	9
in the U.A.E.	5	5	2	317	111*	105.66	93.51	1	2	0	25	13
in West Indies	17	15	4	517	86*	47.00	72.40	0	5	1	31	8
in Zimbabwe	8	8	2	359	114	59.83	81.22	2	1	0	22	7

	Mts	Inns	NO	Runs	Hs	Avg	SR	100	50	0	4s	6s
Home	65	64	8	3528	264	63.00	99.57	11	15	1	342	115
Away	104	99	13	3310	171*	38.48	81.14	10	15	8	267	79
Neutral	55	54	11	2277	140	52.95	86.64	8	13	4	208	50

Performance in Each Calendar Year

	Mts	Inns	NO	Runs	Hs	Avg	SR	100	50	0	4s	6s
2007	4	3	0	61	52	20.33	82.43	0	1	0	3	1
2008	28	28	7	532	70*	25.33	72.57	0	3	2	43	3
2009	9	7	3	102	43*	25.50	65.80	0	0	1	5	1
2010	15	14	1	504	114	38.76	86.00	2	1	2	34	7
2011	16	16	5	611	95	55.54	82.67	0	6	0	40	9
2012	14	13	0	168	68	12.92	66.93	0	1	3	12	2
2013	28	27	4	1196	209	52.00	80.81	2	8	0	119	30
2014	12	12	1	578	264	52.54	94.29	1	3	0	58	22
2015	17	17	1	815	150	50.93	95.43	3	4	2	75	23
2016	10	10	1	564	171*	62.66	95.27	2	2	0	46	19
2017	21	21	3	1293	208*	71.83	99.46	6	5	1	116	46
2018	19	19	5	1030	162	73.57	100.09	5	3	1	104	39
2019	28	27	1	1490	159	57.30	89.92	7	6	1	146	36
2020	3	3	0	171	119	57.00	91.44	1	0	0	16	6

Performance at Each Position

	Mts	Inns	NO	Runs	Hs	Avg	SR	100	50	0	4s	6s
1st position	111	111	13	5527	209	56.39	90.06	19	26	5	510	174
2nd position	27	27	2	1621	264	64.84	100.68	8	5	0	172	47
3rd position	9	9	1	120	26	15.00	62.50	0	0	1	11	1
4th position	26	26	3	715	114	31.08	78.14	2	3	4	51	10
5th position	25	25	6	862	95	45.36	82.64	0	8	2	55	12
6th position	12	12	5	200	58	28.57	73.80	0	1	1	13	0
7th position	7	7	2	70	32	14.00	85.36	0	0	0	5	0

Performance as Player / Captain

	Mts	Inns	NO	Runs	Hs	Avg	SR	100	50	0	4s	6s
as a player	214	207	29	8572	264	48.15	88.44	27	41	13	779	218
as a captain	10	10	3	543	208*	77.57	97.31	2	2	0	38	26

Performance in Each Match Innings

	Mts	Inns	NO	Runs	Hs	Avg	SR	100	50	0	4s	6s
1st match innings	92	91	8	4147	264	49.96	92.29	15	15	7	367	116
2nd match innings	132	126	24	4968	152*	48.70	86.29	14	28	6	450	128

Performance in Won/Lost/Tied/No Result matches

	Mts	Inns	NO	Runs	Hs	Avg	SR	100	50	0	4s	6s
in Won matches	136	132	27	6359	264	60.56	91.82	22	28	7	591	173
in Lost matches	78	78	3	2660	171*	35.46	83.30	7	15	5	216	67
in Tied matches	3	3	0	58	39	19.33	79.45	0	0	0	4	4
in No Result matches	7	4	2	38	29	19.00	64.40	0	0	1	6	0

Performance in Day/Day-Night Matches

	Mts	Inns	NO	Runs	Hs	Avg	SR	100	50	0	4s	6s
Day matches	77	74	17	3341	171*	58.61	86.66	13	16	3	295	77
Day/night matches	147	143	15	5774	264	45.10	90.28	16	27	10	522	167

ROHIT SHARMA IN TWENTY20 INTERNATIONALS

Performance in Each Match

Date	Against	Venue	Batting	Bowling	Fielding
19-09-2007	England	Durban			1 ct
20-09-2007	South Africa	Durban	50* (40)		
22-09-2007	Australia	Durban	8* (5)		
24-09-2007	Pakistan	Johannesburg	30* (16)		1 ct
20-10-2007	Australia	Mumbai BS			
01-02-2008	Australia	Melbourne	8 (8)		
10-02-2009	Sri Lanka	Colombo RPS	4 (11)		
25-02-2009	New Zealand	Christchurch	7 (7)		
06-06-2009	Bangladesh	Nottingham	36 (23)		
10-06-2009	Ireland	Nottingham	52* (45)		
12-06-2009	West Indies	Lord's	5 (3)		
14-06-2009	England	Lord's	9 (8)		
16-06-2009	South Africa	Nottingham	29 (28)	0-15 (2)	

Date	Against	Venue	Batting	Bowling	Fielding
09-12-2009	Sri Lanka	Nagpur	3 (4)	1-22 (3)	
07-05-2010	Australia	Bridgetown	79* (46)		
09-05-2010	West Indies	Bridgetown	5 (8)		2 cts
11-05-2010	Sri Lanka	Gros Islet			
12-06-2010	Zimbabwe	Harare	10 (15)		1 ct
13-06-2010	Zimbabwe	Harare	0* (0)		1 ct
09-01-2011	South Africa	Durban	53 (34)		1 ct
04-06-2011	West Indies	Port-of-Spain	26 (23)		
31-08-2011	England	Manchester	1 (3)	0-16 (1)	1 ct
01-02-2012	Australia	Sydney ANZ	0 (1)	0-2 (0.2)	
03-02-2012	Australia	Melbourne			
30-03-2012	South Africa	Johannesburg		0-14 (1)	3 cts
07-08-2012	Sri Lanka	Pallekele		0-9 (1)	
11-09-2012	New Zealand	Chennai	4* (2)		
19-09-2012	Afghanistan	Colombo RPS	1* (1)	0-10 (1)	1 ct
23-09-2012	England	Colombo RPS	55* (33)		
28-09-2012	Australia	Colombo RPS	1 (2)	0-12 (1)	
30-09-2012	Pakistan	Colombo RPS			1 ct
02-10-2012	South Africa	Colombo RPS	25 (27)	0-13 (1)	1 ct
22-12-2012	England	Mumbai WS	24 (19)		
25-12-2012	Pakistan	Bangalore	2 (2)		
28-12-2012	Pakistan	Ahmedabad	4* (2)		1 ct
10-10-2013	Australia	Rajkot	8 (8)		
21-03-2014	Pakistan	Mirpur	24 (21)		
23-03-2014	West Indies	Mirpur	62* (55)		1 ct
28-03-2014	Bangladesh	Mirpur	56 (44)		1 ct
30-03-2014	Australia	Mirpur	5 (3)		1 ct
04-04-2014	South Africa	Mirpur	24 (13)		1 ct
06-04-2014	Sri Lanka	Mirpur	29 (26)		
02-10-2015	South Africa	Dharamsala	106 (66)		
05-10-2015	South Africa	Cuttack	22 (24)		1 ct
26-01-2016	Australia	Adelaide	31 (20)		

Date	Against	Venue	Batting	Bowling	Fielding
29-01-2016	Australia	Melbourne	60 (47)		
31-01-2016	Australia	Sydney	52 (38)		
09-02-2016	Sri Lanka	Pune	0 (2)		
12-02-2016	Sri Lanka	Ranchi	43 (36)		
14-02-2016	Sri Lanka	Visakhapatnam	13 (13)		
24-02-2016	Bangladesh	Mirpur	83 (55)		1 ct
27-02-2016	Pakistan	Mirpur	0 (2)		
01-03-2016	Sri Lanka	Mirpur	15 (14)		
03-03-2016	UAE	Mirpur	39 (28)		
06-03-2016	Bangladesh	Mirpur	1 (5)		
15-03-2016	New Zealand	Nagpur	5 (7)		
19-03-2016	Pakistan	Kolkata	10 (11)		
23-03-2016	Bangladesh	Bangalore	18 (16)		
27-03-2016	Australia	Mohali	12 (17)		
31-03-2016	West Indies	Mumbai WS	43 (31)		1 ct
27-08-2016	West Indies	Lauderhill	62 (28)		
28-08-2016	West Indies	Lauderhill	10* (8)		
06-09-2017	Sri Lanka	Colombo RPS	9 (8)		
07-10-2017	Australia	Ranchi	11 (7)		
10-10-2017	Australia	Guwahati	8 (4)		
01-11-2017	New Zealand	Delhi	80 (55)		1 ct
04-11-2017	New Zealand	Rajkot	5 (6)		1 ct
07-11-2017	New Zealand	Karyavattom	8 (9)		1 ct
20-12-2017	Sri Lanka	Cuttack	17 (13)		
22-12-2017	Sri Lanka	Indore	118 (43)		
24-12-2017	Sri Lanka	Mumbai WS	27 (20)		1 ct
18-02-2018	South Africa	Johannesburg	21 (9)		
21-02-2018	South Africa	Centurion	0 (1)		
24-02-2018	South Africa	Cape Town	11 (8)		2 cts
06-03-2018	Sri Lanka	Colombo RPS	0 (4)		
08-03-2018	Bangladesh	Colombo RPS	17 (13)		
12-03-2018	Sri Lanka	Colombo RPS	11 (7)		1 ct
14-03-2018	Bangladesh	Colombo RPS	89 (61)		
18-03-2018	Bangladesh	Colombo RPS	56 (42)		
27-06-2018	Ireland	Dublin	97 (61)		
29-06-2018	Ireland	Dublin	0 (2)		
03-07-2018	England	Manchester	32 (30)		

Date	Against	Venue	Batting	Bowling	Fielding
06-07-2018	England	Cardiff	5 (9)		
08-07-2018	England	Bristol	100* (56)		
04-11-2018	West Indies	Kolkata	6 (6)		
06-11-2018	West Indies	Lucknow	111* (61)		3 cts
11-11-2018	West Indies	Chennai	4 (6)		
21-11-2018	Australia	Brisbane	7 (8)		
23-11-2018	Australia	Melbourne			
25-11-2018	Australia	Sydney	23 (16)		1 ct
06-02-2019	New Zealand	Wellington	1 (5)		
08-02-2019	New Zealand	Auckland	50 (29)		2 cts
10-02-2019	New Zealand	Hamilton	38 (32)		
24-02-2019	Australia	Visakhapatnam	5 (8)		
03-08-2019	West Indies	Lauderhill	24 (25)		
04-08-2019	West Indies	Lauderhill	67 (51)		
18-09-2019	South Africa	Mohali	12 (12)		–
22-09-2019	South Africa	Bangalore	9 (8)		
03-11-2019	Bangladesh	Delhi	9 (5)		
07-11-2019	Bangladesh	Rajkot	85 (43)		1 ct
10-11-2019	Bangladesh	Nagpur	2 (6)		
06-12-2019	West Indies	Hyderabad	8 (10)		2 cts
08-12-2019	West Indies	Karyavattom	15 (18)		
11-12-2019	West Indies	Mumbai WS	71 (34)		
24-01-2020	New Zealand	Auckland	7 (6)		1 ct
26-01-2020	New Zealand	Auckland	8 (6)		1 ct
29-01-2020	New Zealand	Hamilton	65 (40)		
02-02-2020	New Zealand	Mount Maunganui	60* (41)		

Innings Break-up

Runs	Innings
0	7
1-9	34
10-29	26
30-49	8
50-89	20
90-99	1
100+	4

Mode of Dismissals

	Innings
caught in the field	45
caught by keeper	8
bowled	15
leg before wicket	9
run out	5
stumped	3
hit wicket	0
completed innings	85
(not out)	15

Performance Against Each Country

	Mts	Inns	NO	Runs	Hs	Avg	SR	100	50	0	4s	6s
vs Afghanistan	1	1	1	1	1*	-	100.00	0	0	0	0	0
vs Australia	19	16	2	318	79*	22.71	133.61	0	3	1	25	15
vs Bangladesh	11	11	0	452	89	41.09	144.40	0	5	0	36	21
vs England	8	7	2	226	100*	45.20	143.03	1	1	0	22	8
vs Ireland	3	3	1	149	97	74.50	137.96	0	2	1	12	6
vs New Zealand	13	13	2	338	80	30.72	137.95	0	4	0	25	16
vs Pakistan	7	6	2	70	30*	17.50	129.62	0	0	1	6	3
vs South Africa	13	12	1	362	106	32.90	134.07	1	2	1	41	14
vs Sri Lanka	15	13	0	289	118	22.23	143.78	1	0	2	29	14
vs U.A.E.	1	1	0	39	39	39.00	139.28	0	0	0	7	1
vs West Indies	15	15	3	519	111*	43.25	141.41	1	4	0	41	29
vs Zimbabwe	2	2	1	10	10	10.00	66.66	0	0	0	1	0
TOTAL	108	100	15	2773	118	32.62	138.78	4	21	6	245	127

Performance in Each Country

	Mts	Inns	NO	Runs	Hs	Avg	SR	100	50	0	4s	6s
in Australia	9	7	0	181	60	25.85	131.15	0	2	1	16	6
in Bangladesh	11	11	1	338	83	33.80	127.06	0	3	1	36	10
in England	9	9	2	269	100*	38.42	131.21	1	1	0	27	9
in India	37	36	3	928	118	28.12	146.37	3	3	1	84	49

	Mts	Inns	NO	Runs	Hs	Avg	SR	100	50	0	4s	6s
in Ireland	2	2	0	97	97	48.50	153.96	0	1	1	8	5
in New Zealand	8	8	1	236	65	33.71	142.16	0	3	0	17	12
in South Africa	9	7	3	173	53	43.25	153.09	0	2	1	18	8
in Sri Lanka	13	11	2	268	89	29.77	128.22	0	3	1	21	10
in the U.S.A.	4	4	1	163	67	54.33	145.53	0	2	0	12	10
in West Indies	4	3	1	110	79*	55.00	142.85	0	1	0	5	8
in Zimbabwe	2	2	1	10	10	10.00	66.66	0	0	0	1	0

	Mts	Inns	NO	Runs	Hs	Avg	SR	100	50	0	4s	6s
Home	37	36	3	928	118	28.12	146.37	3	3	1	84	49
Away	42	38	4	1001	100*	29.44	134.36	1	10	4	89	42
Neutral	29	26	8	844	89	46.88	136.34	0	8	1	72	36

Performance in Each Calendar Year

	Mts	Inns	NO	Runs	Hs	Avg	SR	100	50	0	4s	6s
2007	5	3	3	88	50*	-	144.26	0	1	0	9	4
2008	1	1	0	8	8	8.00	100.00	0	0	0	1	0
2009	8	8	1	145	52*	20.71	112.40	0	1	0	12	4
2010	5	4	2	94	79*	47.00	136.23	0	1	0	6	6
2011	3	3	0	80	53	26.66	133.33	0	1	0	5	4
2012	13	9	4	116	55*	23.20	130.33	0	1	1	9	2
2013	1	1	0	8	8	8.00	100.00	0	0	0	0	1
2014	6	6	1	200	62*	40.00	123.45	0	2	0	19	6
2015	2	2	0	128	106	64.00	142.22	1	0	0	14	5
2016	18	18	1	497	83	29.23	131.48	0	4	2	45	19
2017	9	9	0	283	118	31.44	171.51	1	1	0	30	16
2018	19	18	2	590	111*	36.87	147.50	2	3	3	51	31
2019	14	14	0	396	85	28.28	138.46	0	4	0	33	22
2020	4	4	1	140	65	46.66	150.53	0	2	0	11	7

Performance at Each Position

	Mts	Inns	NO	Runs	Hs	Avg	SR	100	50	0	4s	6s
1st position	63	63	4	2028	118	34.37	144.23	4	14	3	184	100
2nd position	12	12	1	285	56	25.90	118.75	0	2	1	28	7
3rd position	2	2	1	113	60*	113.00	150.66	0	2	0	8	5
4th position	7	7	2	181	79*	36.20	131.15	0	2	1	13	8
5th position	8	8	2	87	50*	14.50	112.98	0	1	1	9	3
6th position	5	5	3	72	30*	36.00	126.31	0	0	0	2	4
7th position	3	3	2	7	4*	7.00	140.00	0	0	0	1	0

Performance as Player/Captain

	Mts	Inns	NO	Runs	Hs	Avg	SR	100	50	0	4s	6s
as a player	89	81	13	2061	106	30.30	132.71	2	16	5	185	87
as a captain	19	19	2	712	118	41.88	160.00	2	5	1	60	40

Performance in Each Match Innings

	Inns	NO	Runs	Hs	Avg	SR	100	50	0	4s	6s
1st match innings	51	8	1644	118	38.23	146.13	3	12	4	144	76
2nd match innings	49	7	1129	100*	26.88	129.32	1	9	2	101	51

Performance in Won/Lost/No Result Matches

	Mts	Inns	NO	Runs	Hs	Avg	SR	100	50	0	4s	6s
in Won matches	70	65	12	2152	118	40.60	141.85	3	18	2	190	103
in Lost matches	35	33	2	546	106	17.61	126.09	1	2	4	49	20
in Tied matches	1	1	0	65	65	65.00	162.50	0	1	0	6	3
in No Result matches	2	1	1	10	10*	-	125.00	0	0	0	0	1

Note: All statistics are updated before the start of IPL2020.

Rohit Sharma Career Highlights

– RAJNEESH GUPTA

TEST CRICKET

One of the 15 Indian batsmen to have scored a hundred on Test debut (177 vs West Indies at Kolkata in 2013–2014).

Indian Batsmen Scoring a Hundred on Test debut

Player	Inns1	Inns2	Vs	Venue	Season
Lala Amarnath	38	118	Eng	Bombay Gym	1933-34
Deepak Shodhan	110	–	Pak	Calcutta	1952-53
AG Kripal Singh	100*	–	NZ	Hyderabad	1955-56
Abbas Ali Baig	26	112	Eng	Manchester	1959
Hanumant Singh	105	23	Eng	Delhi	1963-64
Gundappa Viswanath	0	137	Aus	Kanpur	1969-70
Surinder Amarnath	124	9	NZ	Auckland	1975-76
Mohammad Azharuddin	110	–	Eng	Calcutta	1984-85
Pravin Amre	103	–	SA	Durban	1992-93
Sourav Ganguly	131	–	Eng	Lord's	1996
Virender Sehwag	105	31	SA	Bloemfontein	2001-02
Suresh Raina	120	–	SL	Colombo SSC	2010
Shikhar Dhawan	187	–	Aus	Mohali	2012-13
Rohit Sharma	177	–	WI	Kolkata	2013-14
Prithvi Shaw	134	–	WI	Rajkot	2018-19

Rohit's 177 is the highest score by a Test debutant at number six.

Highest Individual Scores at # 6 on Test Debut

Batsman	Runs	For	Vs	Venue	Season
Rohit Sharma	177	Ind	WI	Kolkata	2013-14
Doug Walters	155	Aus	Eng	Brisbane	1965-66
Michael Clarke	151	Aus	Ind	Bangalore	2004-05
Mark Waugh	138	Aus	Eng	Adelaide	1990-91
Bryan Valentine	136	Eng	Ind	Bombay Gym	1933-34
Kane Williamson	131	NZ	Ind	Ahmedabad	2010-11

Rohit's 177 is the second highest score by an Indian on Test debut after Shikhar Dhawan's 187 against Australia at Mohali in 2012–2013 and the seventh highest individual score by a player batting for the first time in Test cricket.

Highest Scores in the First Test innings

	Score	For	Vs	Venue	Season
'Tip' Foster	287	Eng	Aus	Sydney	1903-04
Jacobus Rudolph	222*	SA	Ban	Chittagong	2002-03
Mathew Sinclair	214	NZ	WI	Wellington	1999-00
Lawrence Rowe	214	WI	NZ	Kingston	1971-72
Brendon Kuruppu	201*	SL	NZ	Colombo CCC	1986-87
Shikhar Dhawan	187	Ind	Aus	Mohali	2012-13
Rohit Sharma	177	Ind	WI	Kolkata	2013-14
Hamish Rutherford	171	NZ	Eng	Dunedin	2012-13
Yasir Hameed	170	Pak	Ban	Karachi	2003
Khalid Ibadulla	166	Pak	Aus	Karachi	1964-65

Rohit made his Test debut after having appeared in 108 one-day internationals, which made him the first player ever to make his Test debut after appearing in more than 100 one-day internationals.

By making an unbeaten 111 in his second Test (at the Wankhede), Rohit joined a select band of players scoring hundreds in their first two Test innings, with only one other Indian in this illustrious list.

Players Scoring Hundreds in First Two Test Innings

Player	Runs	Opponent	Venue	Season
Lawrence Rowe (WI)	214	New Zealand	Kingston	1971-72
	100*			
Alvin Kallicharran (WI)	100*	New Zealand	Georgetown	1971-72
	101		Port of Spain	
Sourav Ganguly (Ind)	131	England	Lord's	1996
	136		Nottingham	
Yasir Hameed (Pak)	170	Bangladesh	Karachi	2003
	105			
Rohit Sharma (Ind)	177	West Indies	Kolkata	2013-14
	111*		Mumbai WS	

Between 2016–2017 and 2019–2020 Rohit Sharma scored at least a fifty in seven consecutive innings in Tests on the Indian soil—the most for any player. Rohit's sequence: 82 at Kolkata and 51* at Indore vs NZ in 2016–2017; 102* at Nagpur, and 65 & 50* at Delhi vs SL in 2017–2018; and 176 & 127 at Visakhapatnam vs SA in 2019–2020. Before him, three other batsmen had managed to score six 50s in a row.

Most Consecutive Fifty-Plus Scores in Tests on Indian Soil

50+ Scores	Batsman	For	100s	50s	Period
7	Rohit Sharma	India	3	4	2016-17 to 2019-20
6	Everton Weekes	West Indies	4	2	1948-49
6	Rahul Dravid	India	0	6	1997-98
6	Andy Flower	Zimbabwe	3	3	1992-93 to 2000-01

Opening the innings for the first time in a Test against South Africa at Visakhapatnam in 2019–2020, Rohit made 176 in the first innings. He thus became only the fourth Indian batsman to score a century in

his maiden innings as an opener in Test cricket after Shikhar Dhawan, K.L. Rahul and Prithvi Shaw. Rohit's 176 is the fourth highest score by a player in his maiden innings as an opener.

Highest Score in Maiden Innings as Opener in Tests

Player	Score	For	Vs	Venue	Season
Brendon Kuruppu	201*	SL	NZ	Colombo CCC	1986-87
Graeme Smith	200	SA	Ban	East London	2002-03
Shikhar Dhawan	187	Ind	Aus	Mohali	2012-13
Rohit Sharma	176	Ind	SA	Visakhapatnam	2019-20
Hamish Rutherford	171	NZ	Eng	Dunedin	2012-13

By scoring 127 in the second innings of Visakhapatnam Test, Rohit became the sixth Indian batsman to score hundreds in each innings of a Test match emulating Vijay Hazare, Sunil Gavaskar (thrice), Rahul Dravid (twice), Virat Kohli and Ajinkya Rahane. He is only the second after Sunil Gavaskar to do so while opening the innings for India.

Hundred in Each Innings of a Test for India

Player	Inns1	Inns2	Vs	Venue	Season
Vijay Hazare	116	145	Aus	Adelaide	1947-48
Sunil Gavaskar †	124	220	WI	Port of Spain	1970-71
Sunil Gavaskar †	111	137	Pak	Karachi	1978-79
Sunil Gavaskar †	107	182*	WI	Kolkata	1978-79
Rahul Dravid	190	103*	NZ	Hamilton	1998-99
Rahul Dravid	110	135	Pak	Kolkata	2004-05
Virat Kohli	115	141	Aus	Adelaide	2014-15
Ajinkya Rahane	127	100*	SA	Delhi	2015-16
Rohit Sharma †	176	127	SA	Visakhapatnam	2019-20

† as an opener

Rohit's 303 runs in the Visakhapatnam Test are the most by a player in his maiden Test as an opener. Rohit also became the first to score hundreds in each innings of his maiden Test as an opener.

Rohit's 13 sixes in the Visakhapatnam Test (six in the first innings and seven in the second) are the most by a batsman in a Test match. Rohit is, in fact, the only player to have hit six sixes in both innings of a Test match.

Most Sixes in a Test by a Player

Sixes	Inns1	Inns2	Player	Opponent	Venue	Season
13	6	7	Rohit Sharma (Ind)	South Africa	Visakhapatnam	2019-20
12	12	–	Wasim Akram (Pak)	Zimbabwe	Sheikhupura	1996-97
11	0	11	Nathan Astle (NZ)	England	Christchurch	2001-02
11	11	–	Matthew Hayden (Aus)	Zimbabwe	Perth	2003-04
11	11	–	Brendon McCullum (NZ)	Pakistan	Sharjah	2014-15
11	11	–	Brendon McCullum (NZ)	Sri Lanka	Christchurch	2014-15
11	11	0	Ben Stokes (Eng)	South Africa	Cape Town	2015-16

Rohit scored 212 off 255 balls in the third Test of 2019–2020 series against South Africa—in his fourth innings as an opener. The four innings are the fewest by an Indian for a double hundred as an opener.

Fewest Innings Taken to Score a Double Hundred as an Opener

Innings	Test #	Batsman	Score	Opponent	Venue	Season
1	1	Brendon Kuruppu (SL)	201*	New Zealand	Colombo CCC	1986-87
1	3	Graeme Smith (SA)	200	Bangladesh	East London	2002-03
2	4	Sid Barnes (Aus)	234	England	Sydney	1946-47

Innings	Test #	Batsman	Score	Opponent	Venue	Season
2	2	David Lloyd (Eng)	214*	India	Birmingham	1974
4	10	Lawrence Rowe (WI)	302	England	Bridgetown	1973-74
4	3	Aamer Sohail (Pak)	205	England	Manchester	1992
4	30	Rohit Sharma (Ind)	212	South Africa	Ranchi	2019-20

Rohit Sharma is the only Indian to have reached his 100 and 200 with a six in the same innings in Tests. He did so against South Africa at Ranchi in 2019–2020 when he completed his hundred with a six off David Piedt and his double hundred with a six off Lungi Ngidi.

Rohit's 19 sixes in the 2019–2020 series against South Africa are the most by a batsman in a Test series.

Most Sixes Hit by a Batsman in a Test Series

Sixes	Batsman	Opponent	Tests	Innings	Season
19	Rohit Sharma (Ind)	South Africa	3	4	2019-20
15	Shimron Hetmyer (WI)	Bangladesh	2	4	2018-19

Among all batsmen who have played at least 10 innings at home, Rohit's batting average of 88.33 is the second highest after Don Bradman.

Most Successful Batsmen in Home Tests (Min. 10 innings)

Avg	Player	Mts	Inns	NO	Runs	Hs	100	50
98.22	Don Bradman (Aus)	33	50	6	4322	299*	18	10
88.33	Rohit Sharma (Ind)	14	20	5	1325	212	6	5
86.25	Adam Voges (Aus)	8	12	4	690	269*	3	1
85.41	Marnus Labuschagne (Aus)	8	12	0	1025	215	4	4
81.66	Douglas Jardine (Eng)	8	10	4	490	127	1	3

Avg	Player	Mts	Inns	NO	Runs	Hs	100	50
77.56	George Headley (WI)	10	18	2	1241	270*	5	2
75.78	Bob Cowper (Aus)	9	14	0	1061	307	3	5
71.14	Steve Smith (Aus)	34	57	10	3344	239	13	12
69.83	Clyde Walcott (WI)	25	42	5	2584	220	11	9
69.56	Vijay Hazare (Ind)	13	20	4	1113	164*	5	4

ONE-DAY INTERNATIONALS

- Holds the record of the highest individual score in the ODIs with 264 against Sri Lanka at Kolkata in 2014
- Only player to hit more than one double hundred, having passed the 200-mark on three separate occasions
- Only player with eight scores of 150 or more in the ODIs
- Holds the record of scoring most boundaries (fours and sixes) in an innings—186 during his 264
- Quickest to hit 200 sixes in the ODIs (in terms of innings)
- Holds the record of most sixes by an Indian in the ODIs (244)
- Only two Indians have scored more ODI centuries than Rohit's 29—Sachin Tendulkar (49) and Virat Kohli (43)
- The highest individual ODI score for India in 2013—209 vs Australia at Bangalore
- The highest individual ODI score for India in 2014—264 vs Sri Lanka at Kolkata (world record)
- The highest individual ODI score for India in 2015—150 vs South Africa at Kanpur
- The highest individual ODI score for India in 2016—171* vs Australia at Perth
- The highest individual ODI score for India in 2017—208* vs Sri Lanka at Mohali

- The highest individual ODI score for India in 2018—162 vs West Indies at Mumbai BS
- The highest individual ODI score for India in 2019—159 vs West Indies at Visakhapatnam
- Scored five centuries in World Cup 2019, most by any batsman in a single edition. This also established a new record of most hundreds in an ODI series/tournament.

Most Hundreds in an ODI Tournament/Series

100s	Player	Tournament	Scores
5	Rohit Sharma (Ind)	World Cup 2019	122* vs South Africa
			140 vs Pakistan
			102 vs England
			104 vs Bangladesh
			103 vs Sri Lanka
4	Kumar Sangakkara (SL)	World Cup 2015	105* vs Bangladesh
			117* vs England
			104 vs Australia
			124 vs Scotland

- The six hundreds by Rohit in the World Cup (one in 2015 and five in 2019) are the joint-most by any batsman in the tournament's history.

Most Hundreds in the World Cup

100s	Player	Inns	Inns / 100
6	Rohit Sharma (Ind)	17	2.83
6	Sachin Tendulkar (Ind)	44	7.33
5	Kumar Sangakkara (SL)	35	7.00
5	Ricky Ponting (Aus)	42	8.40

- Rohit's tally of 648 runs in the 2019 edition are the third most by any player in a single edition of the World Cup.

Most Runs in a Single Edition of World Cup

Player	Year	Inns	Runs	Hs	Avg	SR	100	50
Sachin Tendulkar (Ind)	2003	11	673	152	61.18	89.25	1	6
Matthew Hayden (Aus)	2007	10	659	158	73.22	101.07	3	1
Rohit Sharma (Ind)	2019	9	648	140	81.00	98.33	5	1
David Warner (Aus)	2019	10	647	166	71.88	89.36	3	3
Shakib Al Hasan (Ban)	2019	8	606	124*	86.57	96.03	2	5

- Rohit shares the Indian record of scoring 50 or more in most consecutive innings.

Indian Batsmen with Five Consecutive 50+ Scores in ODIs

Player	Year	Scores
Sachin Tendulkar	1994	62, 66, 54, 88 & 105
Virat Kohli	2012	133*, 108, 66, 183 & 106
Virat Kohli	2013	68*, 61, 100*, 68 & 115*
Ajinkya Rahane	2017–2018	55, 70, 53, 61 & 79
Rohit Sharma	2019	95, 56, 122*, 57 & 140
Virat Kohli	2019	82, 77, 67, 72 & 66

- Rohit finished as the highest run-scorer in ODIs in the year 2019 with 1490 runs.
- From his debut in 2007 until the end of 2012, Rohit averaged 30.43 from 86 ODIs; only two hundreds and 12 half-centuries in that period. Since then he has aggregated 7137 runs in 136 innings at an average of 59.47 with 27 hundreds and 31 half-centuries.

Rohit Sharma in ODIs

	Inns	Runs	Hs	Avg	100	50	SR
2007–2012	81	1978	114	30.43	2	12	77.93
2013 onward	136	7137	264	59.47	27	31	92.54
Overall	217	9115	264	49.27	29	43	88.92

- His 46 sixes in 2017 are the most hit by an Indian batsman in the ODIs in a single calendar year.

Most Sixes by Indian Players in ODIs in a Calendar Year

6s	Player	Inns	Balls / Six
46	Rohit Sharma	21	61.90
40	Sachin Tendulkar	33	56.18
39	Rohit Sharma	19	54.16
36	Rohit Sharma	27	61.37
35	Sourav Ganguly	32	59.63

- Rohit's fastest ODI hundred came off 82 balls—vs England at Nottingham in 2018. His slowest came in 128 balls—vs South Africa at Southampton in 2019.
- Between July 2018 and July 2019 Rohit aggregated 2,063 runs in 34 innings with 10 hundreds. No one else has scored 10 hundreds in any span of 365 days in ODIs!

Most 100s in a Span of 365 Days in ODIs

100s	Player	Span	Inns
10	Rohit Sharma (Ind)	Jul 2018 – Jul 2019	34
9	Sachin Tendulkar (Ind)	Dec 1997 – Nov 1998	38
8	David Warner (Aus)	Feb 2016 – Jan 2017	25
8	Hashim Amla (SA)	Jul 2014 – Mar 2015	26
8	Virat Kohli (Ind)	Sep 2011 – Aug 2012	31

- He is the only Indian to score more than the opposition on two occasions. He did so against Sri Lanka at Kolkata in 2014 (Rohit 264, Sri Lanka 251) and against West Indies at Mumbai BS in 2018 (Rohit 162, West Indies 153).

TWENTY20 INTERNATIONALS

- Is the most capped cricketer for India in T20Is, with 108 appearances
- Holds the record of scoring most centuries in the T20Is (4)
- Holds the record of scoring most fifty-plus scores in T20Is (25)

Most Fifty-Plus Scores in T20Is

50+ Scores	Batsman	Country	100s	50s	Mts	Inns
25	Rohit Sharma	India	4	21	108	100
24	Virat Kohli	India	0	24	82	76
19	David Warner	Australia	1	18	80	80
18	Paul Stirling	Ireland	0	18	78	77
17	Martin Guptill	New Zealand	2	15	88	85
15	Chris Gayle	West Indies	2	13	58	54
15	Brendon McCullum	New Zealand	2	13	71	70

- Rohit holds the record of hitting most sixes in T20Is.

Most Sixes in T20 Internationals

6s	Player	Inns	Balls / Six
127	Rohit Sharma (Ind)	100	15.73
119	Martin Guptill (NZ)	85	15.83
111	Eoin Morgan (Eng)	91	14.47
107	Colin Munro (NZ)	62	10.30
105	Chris Gayle (WI)	54	10.85

- Has the second highest run-aggregate in T20Is with 2,773 runs, behind only Virat Kohli (2,794)
- Holds the record of scoring the fastest hundred in this format (jointly with South Africa's David Miller) off 35 balls against Sri Lanka at Indore in 2017
- Holds the record of highest individual score by an Indian in T20Is (118 against Sri Lanka at Indore in 2017)

- Holds the record of hitting most sixes by an Indian in a T20I with 10 sixes in the match against Sri Lanka at Indore in 2017
- Is the only captain to score two hundreds in Twenty20 Internationals
- Rohit made 58.52 per cent of India's total (79* out of 135) against Australia at Bridgetown in 2010—the highest contribution by an Indian player in a T20I innings where the team was dismissed.

ALL INTERNATIONAL CRICKET

- One of the three Indian batsmen to have scored a hundred in all three international formats (Tests, ODIs and T20Is). Rohit is the only one among the three to do so as an opener
  - First Test hundred: 177 vs West Indies, November 2013
  - First ODI hundred: 114 vs Zimbabwe, May 2010
  - First T20 hundred: 106 vs South Africa, October 2015
- First batsman to score three hundreds in each format of international cricket—6 in Tests, 29 in ODIs, 4 in T20Is
- First player to score a hundred in all three formats of the game in a single tour vs Sri Lanka in October–December 2017
- Holds the record of hitting most sixes by an Indian in international cricket

Most Sixes by Indian Players in International Cricket

6s	Player	Inns
423	Rohit Sharma	370
359	MS Dhoni	526
264	Sachin Tendulkar	782
251	Yuvraj Singh	391
247	Sourav Ganguly	488
243	Virender Sehwag	443

Most Sixes in International Cricket

6s	Player	Inns
534	Chris Gayle (WI)	530
476	Shahid Afridi (Pak)	508
423	Rohit Sharma (Ind)	370
398	Brendon McCullum (NZ)	474
359	MS Dhoni (Ind)	526
352	Sanath Jayasuriya (SL)	651

- Rohit holds the record of hitting most sixes in international cricket played in India.

Most Sixes in International Cricket in India

6s	Player	Inns
197	Rohit Sharma	120
186	MS Dhoni	208
113	Yuvraj Singh	153
111	Virender Sehwag	179
110	Virat Kohli	183
107	Sachin Tendulkar	313

- He holds the record of hitting maximum sixes in the international cricket in a calendar year. In fact, Rohit has been the leading six-hitter in each of the last three years!

Most Sixes in International Cricket in a Single Year

6s	Player	Year
78	Rohit Sharma (Ind)	2019
74	Rohit Sharma (Ind)	2018
65	Rohit Sharma (Ind)	2017
63	AB de Villiers (SA)	2015
60	Eoin Morgan (Eng)	2019

MISCELLANEOUS

- First Indian batsman to score a T20 hundred. Playing for Mumbai against Gujarat in 2006–2007 Syed Mushtaq Ali Trophy (Inter State Twenty-20 Tournament) Rohit made 101* off 45 balls
- Holds the record of scoring most (6) hundreds by an Indian in T20 cricket
- Holds the record of scoring most (361) sixes hit by an Indian in T20 cricket
- Has the second highest run-aggregate by an Indian in T20 cricket with 8,642 runs. Only Virat Kohli has scored more (8,900)
- Has never lost an IPL final, winning 5 out of 5. Rohit won his first title with Deccan Chargers in 2009. In 2013, Rohit won his first title as captain when he led Mumbai Indians to their first title. Rohit repeated the feat in 2015, 2017 and 2019 and maintained a perfect record in the IPL final
- Has won 9 out of 10 T20 finals in his career. Apart from the five IPL finals, Rohit won the World T20 in 2007 with India, the Champions League 2013 with Mumbai Indians, the Asia Cup in 2016 with India and the Nidahas Trophy in 2018. The only loss in a final came in 2014 World T20
- Has the third highest run-aggregate in the IPL with 4,898 with one hundred. Only Virat Kohli and Suresh Raina are ahead of him
- One of the most successful captains in the IPL with 62 wins in 104 matches
- Took a T20 hat-trick against the Mumbai Indians in 2009

About the Authors

Vijay Lokapally is a well-travelled journalist, author and former Deputy Editor of *The Hindu* and *Sportstar*.

Respected for his enviable access to cricketers, he is renowned for reporting extensively on various issues of sporting and cultural importance. Lokapally has been covering sports for *The Hindu* and *Sportstar* since 1986.

He is a passionate lover and student of cricket. He covered his first Test in 1981 as a freelancer and has gone on to cover six limited-over World Cups and more than 100 Tests and One Day Internationals.

A committed journalist, Lokapally is credited with writing acclaimed books: *World Cup Warriors: The Boys in Blue, Driven: The Virat Kohli Story* and *The Virender Sehwag Story*.

Lokapally lives in New Delhi with his wife Sunanda and son Akshay.

G. Krishnan has been a sports journalist for more than two decades. While he has reported on a wide range of competitive games, his major contributions have been in cricket writing.

Passionate about sports in general and cricket in particular, Krishnan, known as 'Gikku' among friends, has even tried his hand at umpiring from 1997 to 1999 before pursuing sports journalism. He covered sports for *Deccan Herald*, *Hindustan Times* and *DNA*. He is now an independent sports journalist, and regularly blogs at https://gikkusports.wordpress.com/.

Krishnan lives in Mumbai with his wife Priya and son Aman.

The Hitman: The Rohit Sharma Story is Krishnan's first book.

Rajneesh Gupta is a seasoned cricket statistician with over twenty-five years of compiling and working on cricket statistics spread over print and electronic media. He has worked with leading sports channels/ production houses covering all major cricket tournaments live for TV, including Cricket World Cups, World T20, Champions Trophy, IPL, CLT20 and many other series/tournaments. His articles have been featured in almost all leading newspapers, cricket magazines in India. His research work has been published in *Wisden Cricketers' Almanack*, *Wisden India*, *Indian Cricket*, etc. He has provided statistical sections for numerous books on cricket.